YOU'RE HIRED!
FIND WORK AT 50+

YOU'RE HIRED! GUIDES

Assessment Centres: Essential advice for peak performance

CV: How to write a brilliant CV

CVs, Interview Answers & Psychometric Tests

Find Work at 50+: A positive approach to securing the job you want

Interview Answers: Impressive answers to tough questions

Interview: Tips & Techniques for a brilliant interview

Job Hunting Online: The Complete Guide

Psychometric Tests: Proven tactics to help you pass

Total Job Search: How to find and secure your dream job

See our website at www.trotman.co.uk for a comprehensive list of published and forthcoming Trotman titles.

YOU'RE HIRED!
FIND WORK AT 50+

A POSITIVE APPROACH
TO SECURING THE JOB YOU WANT

DENISE TAYLOR

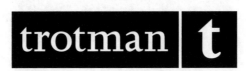

You're Hired! Find Work at 50+: A positive approach to securing the job you want

This first edition published in 2016 by Trotman Publishing, an imprint of Crimson Publishing Ltd, 19–21c Charles Street, Bath, BA1 1HX

© Denise Taylor 2016

Author Denise Taylor

British Library Cataloguing in Publication Data
A catalogue record for this book is available from the British Library

ISBN 978 1 84455 619 9

Please note that all websites given in this book are subject to change so you may find that some of these sites in time may be renamed, merge with other sites or disappear.

Designed by Nicki Averill
Typeset by IDSUK (DataConnection) Ltd
Printed and bound in the UK by Ashford Colour Press, Gosport, Hants

CONTENTS

LIST OF ACTIVITIES

ABOUT THE AUTHOR

Denise Taylor is an award-winning career coach, chartered psychologist, Associate Fellow of the British Psychological Society and a Fellow of the Career Development Institute. She has been helping people find out who they are, what they want to do and to be successful in their job search for more than 20 years. Denise is the founder of Amazing People and noted as one of the top career coaches in the UK with a worldwide client base.

With a combination of educational credentials and vast industry expertise, Denise is renowned for helping clients get results. She has specialised in career development for more than two decades, and has published extensively in this area. Her specialist knowledge is backed up with diplomas in coaching and counselling and master's degrees in occupational psychology from Birkbeck College, University of London and business administration (MBA) from the Open University.

Following a career which saw her rise from Post Office counter clerk to assistant director in less than 14 years, Denise set up Amazing People in 1998. Working predominately with individuals, Denise helps students, graduates and career-changers to define and achieve their employment goals.

Denise is also a sought-after consultant and advises companies as diverse as charities, energy companies and the Civil Service, helping them make accurate recruitment decisions and to provide support in times of redundancy.

Denise was the featured careers coach on ITV's *Tonight* programme – *How Safe is your Job?* She is regularly featured in the media, including as the midnight expert on Radio 5 Live, and called to comment on career issues for national and regional radio. Author of nine books including *How to get a Job in a Recession, Now you've been Shortlisted* and *Introducing Getting the Job you Want.*

Meet Denise online at:

www.amazingpeople.co.uk
www.facebook.com/amazingpeopleUK
Twitter.com/amazingpeople
https://uk.linkedin.com/in/denisetaylor

ACKNOWLEDGEMENTS

There are many people to thank, including clients and family.

I'd particularly like to thank Richard Lane and Rachael Baker for their comments and suggestions with earlier versions of this book, and all the clients who allowed me to include their comments as case studies, especially Anita, Gary, Pat, Phil, Rachael, Richard, Simon, Suzanne and Valerie. Thanks, too, to Simon Drake, Director of Executive Recruitment, Search and Interim, Penna PLC; Jacquie Wiggett, Director of HR and Organisational Development at the Financial Ombudsman Service; John Bennett of BennCo2 Ltd, Christopher D. King of CNWL NHS Trust, Debra Carroll and Lyn Barnham.

With thanks to my family, especially Simon, for their patience and support.

Not forgetting the helpful support from my editor Della Oliver and the editorial team at Trotman.

FOREWORD

by John Lees, author of *How to Get a Job You Love*

No group finds this new economy harder to navigate than the generation which, like me, can remember using old currency. Until relatively recently applying for roles meant fitting in to a clear, formulaic process – a job description, a hard copy advertisement, first and second interviews, job offer. We bought into the myth that a recruitment process done this way would be fair and objective and would filter in people capable of doing the job. Job-searching seemed a mechanical, straightforward process.

As Denise Taylor explores in this valuable new book, the jobs market has changed dramatically. From my perspective, this change has been rapid and dramatic. This isn't just about social media and online applications. The major change is around the way organisations have learnt cheap, effective ways of finding staff without going down the traditional line of published advertisements. Many roles come up through today's very unpredictable mix of word of mouth and social media. Roles which are advertised become candidate magnets, attracting hundreds of applications. Finding an interesting job now requires a mix of relentless investigation, influencing and relationship-building.

So, in just over a decade many jobs seem to have gone underground. They're still there – in fact the UK remained a relatively buoyant place to work during the great recession. The big difference is they are harder to fall across passively. We have to learn to think and act very differently. Denise shows us what that new thinking is all about, demonstrating how people need to look hard at their goals, think about how the market will perceive them, and launch themselves in a very different job campaign.

I'm delighted that Denise has produced a guide for this group, who often feel underprivileged in the job market. Some of this is about mindset rather than economic reality. After all, the people who find it toughest to find work are

16- to 24-year-olds. However, it is true that some organisations are 'young' cultures, and some employers have a clichéd, unthinking view of older workers, who of course offer a great many things their younger counterparts can't – wisdom and staying-power being just two. As Denise points out, workers between 50 and 64 often display high levels of commitment and loyalty, and stay longer on average than workers in the first half of their careers. Workers aged 55+ are therefore very good recruitment and training investments. They're more literate, better connected, and having been around the block a bit know how to solve most workplace problems.

I've written in the past about the problems experienced by older workers, and might have written a book for this age group – but I won't be doing so now as this one covers all the angles – it's a great resource. It's full of savvy, smart career and job-search tips based on a real understanding of what employers are looking for. It's a workbook, which means that you're taken step by step through the reflective and action-planning stages that will push you into being an above-average job-seeker.

If you can remember the Beatles before they broke up and you're scratching your head about the new world of work, this is the book you need.

1 INTRODUCTION

This chapter sets the scene and introduces you to the changing world of work. We will focus on a positive future, whilst addressing concerns. You will learn how to refocus and follow a 21st-century job search.

By the end of this chapter you will:

■ have a clearer understanding of why it's harder to find a job today

■ understand the reasons for taking a different (marketing-focused) approach to your job search and why you need an online presence

■ be open to finding work, including short-term assignments and not just a full-time job

■ appreciate that you must know how you match up to a particular job, you can't be vague

■ understand the importance of measurement and the need to keep on track

■ learn how to address specific stereotypes.

Thanks for choosing this book. I want to help you to find work, and I'll be sharing the same advice I use with my personal clients.

My 50+ clients vary in age, in their background and objectives. As a group we are likely to have a much wider range of experiences and goals than if this book was focused on graduates. So I can't write this for just one person. The 50+ group can cover people of 75 and beyond, people who are in urgent need of income and those who have the luxury of a decent pension but still want to work; they see a life without work as boring and lonely. Work has many benefits – it is good for our physical and mental health and well-being. Many may be in need of a decent income because they still have children at home to support. With people starting families later, they have many more years of family-related living costs, university tuition, and more. Others may have elderly parents to care for, sometimes alongside dependent children.

Some of you may have recently been made redundant after a lifetime in one company or industry, like Valerie. Others may have been out of work for over nine months and were about to give up, like Phil and Gary. Others may be in work and looking for a change of job, possibly even to start a new career, such as Richard and Sue. I'm working with a greater number of people in their fifties who want to leave the stress of a full-on job and take things a little easier. They want to take a slow route down to retirement seeking out a four-day-week job or part-time work, or to become a freelancer ('pre-tirement').

Addressing this up front allows me to manage expectations and helps you take charge of how you use this book. I'd like you to treat this as a resource. You could start at the beginning and work through – that's the process I use with many of my clients. Or feel free to jump into the section/chapter that is most relevant to you at this time. Chapter 6 is a guide for people of 65+, or those who want to phase into retirement.

At 50+ we are not past it and many organisations still value our skills, but there is recognisable discrimination. We need to understand this may occur and have a way to deal with this.

The changing world of work

The world of work has changed. There is much more competition for jobs. Many jobs have disappeared, either due to technological advances (we no longer need large volumes of workers and certain kinds of jobs) or outsourced to another country.

There is less security, less full-time working and more contracting, zero hour contracts and people being underemployed. We need to be ready to accept short-term contracts, consultancy and self-employment.

This book is titled 'find work' and it may be that you need to create your own business. Job Centres are encouraging people to set up their own business, possibly to get people off the unemployment register. Nonetheless, from dog-walking to IT support, you could take charge of your income generation. Later I'm going to share a list of more than 50 ways we could earn money, and this may be the spark to get you started. See Chapter 13, Alternatives to a permanent full-time job.

Being clear on what you want

I regularly talk with people who struggle in their job search. Months have gone by and they still haven't got a job offer, and not surprisingly they are losing motivation and are getting despondent.

Too many people are vague about the type of work they seek; they tell me they are looking for something interesting that pays at least a certain amount. But it is far too vague, for me, and anyone else to help them.

When I ask about their job search approach, I find they are taking a scattergun approach, sending off their CV to any and all jobs that even remotely match their background. If this sounds like you, I want you to **stop, take a break, and start again.**

This break isn't for a holiday, but I want you to take a week away from looking for a job and work on your preparation materials before an active return to your job search.

During this week off I want you to **remove your CV from every online site** and review before you start your job search campaign afresh. Think of it like taking your house off the market, clearing the clutter, painting dark walls neutral and putting plants by the front door. You then get new photos and get the house back on sale.

Chapter 3 will help to focus on your goal – what job you want. But first let's have a look at what you have been doing.

MEASUREMENT

Do you know?

- How many jobs did you apply for in the last 1/3/6 months?
- From this list, how many were a great match for your skills and experience?

- How many first interviews did you get?
- How many second interviews did you get?
- Why didn't you get the job offer?

Make a note and if you haven't been measuring, start now.

Then review how you spent your time. What percentage of your time was spent looking online and applying to job ads; how much time did you spend contacting companies direct?

And now consider your applications.

- To what extent were applications, CV and cover letter tailored to the specific job?
- How much research do you do before applying?
- Do you have a LinkedIn profile with at least 200 connections?
- Do you know at least 20 organisations that you would like to work for?
- Do you know at least one person who works at each of these organisations?
- How many people did you connect with last week?

A lot of questions, but it is important to take stock and understand where you are now, like weighing and measuring yourself before you start your weight-loss campaign.

Case Study

Pat said: 'I found seeking at least 20 organisations hard. It made me think as only four came to mind. This prompted me to look at the list of small businesses based in a building nearby. I've made my first application since starting work here: my current employer was advertising for a different role. I spent a lot of time preparing and had to do that speculatively because it looked like after shortlisting the (Skype) interviews would be at short notice. I wasn't successful but I have no regrets as the topic was interesting and some techniques (e.g. statistics software and coding graphs) I wanted to learn anyway.'

As you work through this book, each chapter will get you to review what you have been doing and to focus on how to make changes to increase your chance of success.

21st-century job search

It may be many years since you have looked for a job, and you may not appreciate how many things have changed.

Now it's less about having generic skills and more about an area of specialism. Employers are looking for people who can demonstrate value from day one in a particular niche. Undertake research to find out what's hot, and use time out of work to get up to speed in a new topic, and demonstrate this knowledge through sharing your knowledge, perhaps through online contributions. More on this in Chapter 10, Promoting yourself and being found.

Recruitment practices have changed a great deal over recent years. There are lots of jobs available, but they aren't on job boards – employers have found more cost-effective ways to publicise job vaccancies.

The old way
- Find jobs in newspapers and register on job sites.
- Create a CV and generic cover letter.
- Submit and await a reply.

The new way

- Be very clear on the job you want and why, plus the type of organisation you want to work in.
- Understand your value and be clear on how you stand out from other applicants.
- Create your publicity material – CV, LinkedIn – and ensure they are 'branded'.
- Develop a job-search (marketing) strategy to cover both online and offline areas.
- Make sure you are found online – LinkedIn and more.
- Prepare for getting in contact – you can speak eloquently and succinctly on what you seek, you are ready for interviews, both face-to-face, phone and via Skype.
- Be proactive – contact companies direct, make contacts.
- Be open to considering alternatives such as short-term assignments.

Using techniques from marketing can seem alien. Many of us don't like selling ourselves but we need to develop these skills to find the hidden employment opportunities and also to make ourselves attractive to the people with the power to offer us a job.

Case Study

Pat said: 'In my previous job search I just applied to advertised posts. Last week I met someone from a local small business who described their struggles lacking IT support. I could make a direct approach to them if I was ready to apply for jobs now.'

Companies now find talent through Google and LinkedIn searches, so your online presence matters. See Chapters 9 and 10.

You are most likely to get your next job by breaking the traditional cycle and tackling your job search in a different way. Move beyond fiddling with your CV and applying for jobs.

That's why I want you to focus on two areas.

1. To work on your mindset and to believe that you can succeed.
2. To follow these new and effective methods.

There are many new techniques including using LinkedIn, and having a focus on key words but you can still use your interpersonal skills for connecting. Too many people have focused almost exclusively on online networking, so your ability to network in person will enhance your chance of success.

Case Study

Many people, like Rachael, are generally lacking in confidence, and the idea of having to ring up company after company and make all these contacts and try to get interviews can be incredibly overwhelming. But she did it, recognising that phoning recruitment agencies and going on the job boards is easy, but it doesn't get the results.

Valerie found the need for social media, competency-based interviews and the need to consider short-term assignments alien. She clearly wanted to be looked after and whilst never really happy in her local government job, it did offer security and the flexibility to take days off with flexitime. Then her job was made redundant.

When applying for jobs Valerie expected written acknowledgement of her application, like in the past; she thought the problem was her age. Whilst ageism can be a problem, and age discrimination in employment is unlawful, **not receiving a reply is the norm these days and has nothing to do with our age.** Many applications go through a computer system using key words, and being targeted to the specific job will help you to get through this first hurdle. Valerie also needed to learn how to use job sites and to focus more on building relationships and contacting companies direct. If you are like Valerie, start at the beginning of this book and follow the process.

Phil had been a company director earning close to a six-figure salary, with company car and more. It was nine months on when he got in touch. He'd not been unduly worried not to have a job offer in the first eight months, but time needs to be used effectively and Phil was not being very effective. He'd exhausted his list of contacts, found few opportunities and his self-esteem and confidence were bruised.

When I first raised looking for a less-senior position to get back into work, he was reluctant. But looking at what was important to him – his values and drivers, he accepted that a drop in status was preferable to no income at all.

We refocused his CV and worked on his interview technique. I'll be sharing more about his approach in relevant chapters. Phil got a new job, not a dream job, and he said he felt like he'd taken two steps back, but this flexibility has got him back into the workplace and he has regained his self-confidence. In a year or so he can renew his job search from a different position, using these modern and effective job-search techniques.

Addressing stereotypes

We need to stand up against prejudice and ageism but we also need to challenge ourselves to stay current – we must not be complacent. As older workers, we have to deal with stereotypes. Too much is in the press around cognitive decline, but we can also call on our experience and use mental shortcuts to help us to be more efficient.

Our age is not our identity. Age is not a barrier to performance. We need to seek out organisations that value our experience and be able to address prejudice full on. If there is resistance to offering you the job, it may not be an environment where you'll be comfortable working, so best to move on.

We need to turn our age into an asset so that potential employers see us as seasoned individuals and a brilliant catch, not as overqualified and over the hill.

It will be a great help if you can identify a job that fits your experience, career goals, strengths and personal fulfilment, and make sure that everything you communicate about yourself emphasises this, not your age.

Many of us are still interested in further development and having interesting jobs – we aren't coasting to retirement. A recent survey said that more than twice as many over-50s (11%) want promotion as want to downshift (4%). Many of us will still be able to work, if we want to, as we reach our eighth decade. It should be for us to decide we are ready to stop, not have it foisted upon us.

But there are still people of our age who put themselves down, sometimes due to lacking confidence. They talk about their senior moments and talk about how they preferred things in the past. They come across as a bit fuddy-duddy and don't do themselves any favours. As with people of all ages some negative comments will be true for some, but we can't have people assuming that these statements are true for all of us.

I will address most of the stereotypes in Chapter 14, Interviews at 50+, but let's also look at why we should get the job.

Make our age an asset

Other cultures see age as wisdom, and many of us have great experience we can call on. But recruiters know that there are some who have coasted through their career, doing the minimum, not bothering about development. At interview you must emphasise how you have developed yourself, how you have used your knowledge in such a way that benefits your organisation. Make it clear how you have worked well with people of different ages and how you have mentored younger colleagues.

Many employers do choose older workers (see Appendix 1) as they find too many young workers lack the right skills and work ethic. They choose to recruit us for many of the following reasons.

We are conscientious and knowledgeable

We have a wider skills base, experience, wisdom and are good at problem-solving. Our understanding of using early versions of word-processing software means that we understand how to create, e.g. styles, to save hours of time, and often have a deeper understanding of Excel and PowerPoint. At 55 we have a working and experience track record of around 30–35 years to offer an organisation whereas a 25-year-old may only have two to five years of junior-level experience. We can also draw on our background and knowledge to guide and develop younger staff. We are less likely to take time off sick.

We are loyal

Most of us are reliable, loyal and motivated. Once recruited we are more likely to stay in the job longer and save our employer costs; younger workers are far more likely to move on. When in work, those aged 50–64 have an average job tenure of 13 years, compared with seven years for those aged 25–49. Workers aged 55+ are five times less likely to change jobs compared to workers aged 20–24 and this directly reduces ongoing recruitment and training costs.

We are good communicators

Generally we will write well and have the confidence to speak up. We have also learnt how to get on with a wide range of people and have the confidence to challenge, although we need to make sure we do this carefully. Over the years rough edges have been smoothed and we have gained emotional maturity. We find it much easier to engage with and influence others.

We know people

With age, we know more people and this can prove highly valuable to the new employer. You may well have contacts with suppliers, potential customers and competitors. Think about who you know that could be valuable to the interviewer.

We can address some of these areas as we apply. We can emphasise our background that is relevant to the job we are applying for and take the emphasis off other areas. We can explain in the cover letter why the job interests us and make sure we include how well we match the job requirements.

IN A NUTSHELL

You now appreciate why you need to:

- understand the need to use modern job-search techniques which includes having an online presence – starting with LinkedIn
- be open to considering a range of options, not just full-time work but also short-term assignments and self-employment

- be very clear how you match up to the job you seek
- use your time between jobs to get familiar with recent changes in your industry
- see your age as an asset and use this in any application and in any communication with others.

BEFORE YOU MOVE ON

- Make a note of three key points you have learnt.

- Make a note of what is the top takeaway, for you, from this chapter.

2 MINDSET

What we believe can affect what happens. Focus on the negative, all the reasons why you won't be successful and you dramatically reduce your chance of success. Just like an athlete you need to focus on your goal – being successful in your job search and getting a job offer.

By the end of this chapter you will:

- have strategies ready to deal with disappointment

- understand why you need to change your thoughts and behaviour

- appreciate the benefits of positive affirmations and use these each day.

Why do some people find it easy to get the job they want while others flounder and give up? A lot of it is down to what goes on inside our heads: when we think we will be successful, we probably will; but if we doubt ourselves, our likelihood of success is low.

In this book I'll get you focused on the type of work you seek. You will be clear on why you should get the job and will take action to get to an interview. Without the belief that you can achieve your goal you may as well not even get started.

It can be easy to focus on all the reasons why you won't get a job and that employers prefer youth. Sometimes we skip over more positive stories. Part of my research for the book has been to find examples of employers who welcome people like us making applications, and I've got some of these listed in Appendix 1.

Dealing with disappointments

We all have disappointments: we don't win the race, we lose out on buying something at an auction, or we have an injury that stops us participating in a game. It's how we respond to that disappointment that matters.

We have to treat each disappointment as a learning experience, and use this to do better next time. We also need to remember that sometimes a decision is outside our control. Just like an actor going for a casting call where the casting director may have an ideal in mind (if we are the wrong build or don't fit the character description, we will never be chosen), so at interview, the job may already be allocated to someone and the company is 'going through the motions', or they want someone with specific experience which wasn't made clear in the job ad, it's not just about our age.

But at 50+ we have to deal with age discrimination, which is very difficult to prove. Yes, there are stories of people who aren't successful, but people at 50+ get job offers, their age hasn't been a barrier. That's why mindset is important. We can also consider the type of organisation to target – smaller ones, those with a 50+ owner are often a good place to focus.

Whatever is going on 'out there' it is also important to focus on what goes on inside us, the thoughts we have that can affect our behaviour. We must focus on the positive, not the negative. Focus on what you have done this week, not the job you weren't shortlisted for. But also recognise where you need to take action. Review what you have done and also where you need to improve.

How are you feeling about your job search?

If we approach the job search and especially the interview as if our age is a huge negative, we may in subtle and not so subtle ways provide evidence to others that this is true. If we meet people and are apologetic about our age and see a gap as bigger than it is, that's what other people will see too.

Rather than just read on, I'd like you to take time to write down how you are feeling about getting a new job. I don't know what you will say – the people I have worked with have very different views. Rachael is feeling excited and enthusiastic about finding a new job. Richard found this activity useful, recognising he can err on the negative side. Gary was less positive at this stage of his job search. The words he used were 'scary' and 'depressing'. He said that if he was honest, he would rather go to the dentist than apply for jobs. So who will be more successful?

Rachael was far more likely to have a positive experience, and she did. She knows that the worst that can happen when she sends off her CV is to hear nothing, but she will focus much more on active job-searching. Rachael knows that being focused on a specific goal will put her well ahead of the competition. She is positive and is ready to make direct approaches to organisations and people.

ACTIVITY 3

FEELINGS

Please write down how you currently feel about your job search.

If you are less than positive and enthusiastic, and if you have been looking for a job for several months, I can appreciate your initial motivation may have waned. But are negative thoughts helping? Simon said, 'I'm too old; they will want someone younger,' and Valerie said, 'They will see me as past my prime.' I had to challenge this to get them to step away from a negative mindset.

As you work through this book I'll help you to get clear on why you should get the job you seek – what makes you marketable – but will also help ensure that your goal is realistic when you compare yourself to others. You will also get lots of tips for how to be more effective at interview in Chapter 14.

Lacking confidence

Losing a job can affect our confidence and can affect us like a bereavement, but coming across as someone who lacks confidence doesn't help. You may need to act confident, especially when you meet people and go to interview. Pretend you are someone with lots to offer and focus on good things rather than the negative. I appreciate that you may be badly affected, and for some this will lead to depression, and affect your health. If this is you, do seek out professional advice.

Positive action

Optimism – visualise your success

Professional athletes visualise winning a gold medal and the race. They don't just think it would be nice to win it but instead they use all their senses. They visualise, they can see themselves on the podium, they hear the roar of the crowd, and they feel the tingling sensation knowing they are a winner; they can taste success. Imagery can help to enhance our motivation and increase our confidence. We can imagine ourselves being effective at interview and really connecting with the people we meet.

Imagine yourself being successful in your job search – it can be a very powerful technique. Think of how you will dress and what the workplace will be like. Imagine yourself at your desk and on the phone, talking with customers or in the field delivering goods and services.

Maybe the image isn't clear at the moment, but try to picture yourself carrying out your ideal job: What will you be wearing? How will you be feeling? What will you do?

Believe you are capable of succeeding. Focus on your past successes, skills and experience and not your age. Richard said this was a motivating and rewarding exercise.

WHY ME?

If you find it hard to visualise, what you might prefer to do is to list all the reasons why you should get the job. You don't have to do it now, but certainly by the time you have completed Chapter 4.

Self-talk
Whether or not we succeed often boils down to what goes on in our heads, the inner self-talk. We need to believe we can succeed, and motivate ourselves with our thoughts.

Our self-talk can be either positive or negative. Negative self-talk is more likely to lead to negative results; positive self-talk leads to positive results and can increase our self-confidence. Too often we fill our heads with statements like:

'Who will want me? I'm too old. I worked for 28 years in the same company, and that's all I know.'

'I'm older than the interviewer and all the other candidates. They'll never hire me.'

'I'm not good enough, I've not heard back from any employers.'

'I will never get hired.'

Our mind then looks for lots of reasons to make this true. If you keep telling yourself that you will fail and that you don't expect to be successful then that's what will happen. The more we repeat phrases like this, the less likely we are to be successful in our job search. You need to think about your self-talk and praise yourself for your achievements.

We can turn statements around, so instead of saying *'I'm being discriminated against because of my age,'* we can say *'I have a lot of skills and experience to offer. I'm up to date with technology and still look good,'* or *'I've got some great experience that an employer can benefit from.'*

Instead of saying *'I'm not comfortable telling people about my strengths,'* turn this to *'I will discuss my achievements at interview so an employer will be clear why I'm the best candidate for the job.'*

Case Study

Phil said: 'I needed to shift the balance between the positive, focused, effective, and the negative, draining destructive thoughts. It's the intentional ones that can be tweaked to increase effectiveness, the unintentional take on a life of their own like weeds in a garden.'

Positive affirmations

Reading positive affirmations can help us to achieve our goals. These are in the present tense and state the goals we want to achieve. For job-searching these will be statements such as:

'I am experienced and qualified for the position.'

'I'm skilled, experienced and can be an asset to an organisation/company.'

'I can get the job I want; age is not important.'

'I know I'm older, but why shouldn't they want to hire me? I'm really good at what I do. I have years of experience keeping the numbers straight and balancing the books, and I'm up to date with the latest technology.'

AFFIRMATIONS

I'd like you to write out these, and others, on postcards and keep them in your purse or wallet and on Post-it notes on the bathroom mirror. Have them in other places where you will see them regularly, and read them out loud many times a day.

This can have a very positive impact on our job search. Repeating a message gets it into our subconscious and has a far more positive outcome than repeating negative comments to ourselves.

Case Study

Suzanne said: 'Having chosen to take redundancy at the age of 53, I agree that having a positive mindset is crucial. Several people have said I have a unique combination of skills and experience. It's important for me to use them and market myself in the most effective way, all the time continuing to believe in myself and what I have to offer.'

Dealing with the negative

We can't be 100% positive, so whenever a negative thought comes into our mind we need to stop the thought from taking over. I find it helpful to both visualise and say out loud the word 'Stop!' I see it as a red stop sign and if I'm alone will say it out loud, or in my head when I'm with others. You could have an elastic band around your wrist and give it a good twang when you think negative thoughts. The sharp pain will stop you thinking these unhelpful thoughts!

Our beliefs can affect our outcomes

If you think you are too old to get a job and that you won't get shortlisted, that's what is likely to happen. We need to have the inner belief that we can make a change and achieve our desired goal. If we expect to fail, we are creating a negative self-fulfilling prophecy. This can lead to our actual failure, which lowers our self-confidence further.

Our beliefs can have a significant impact on outcomes. For example in a clinical trial, patients were given a harmless injection of saline solution but were told it would lead to hair loss. About 35% of the trial sample actually lost their hair! Our mind is that powerful.

Case Study

It took Gary a long time to get his first interview, and when he did he said how uncomfortable he felt as the young interviewers talked about the dynamic culture. He said that he thought they were trying to discourage him. So he took it as a negative. I suggested that his interviewers were more likely to be testing his reaction. Whilst Gary is happy to work with younger people and has done in the past, he never spoke about these examples and had decided they didn't want him.

We must believe we can be successful. This determination keeps us going even when we don't get shortlisted. It keeps us focused knowing that if we put the effort in, we will get there eventually as we learn and move on from setbacks.

Treat your job search as a learning opportunity to increase the chance of success – shrug off setbacks and review what you are doing and look at how to improve for next time.

When you are not successful you need to reflect on the process you have followed, see what hasn't worked and try something different – better preparation, create a stronger CV, make more direct approaches to companies, etc.

If you simply do more of the same, and if what you are doing isn't working, then more of the same will lead to the same lack of result. People often expect something different, but it's insanity to keep doing the same thing and expect different results.

Locus of control
If you feel in control of any decisions you make, rather than being influenced by others, you are likely to have an internal locus of control. You know that success in your job search is down to you and the actions you take. With an

internal locus of control, you are more likely to see setbacks as opportunities to learn from and use this to motivate you to keep going.

Other people have an external locus of control: they feel that decisions and results are outside of their control – they think that 'what will be, will be' and that no matter what they do, it won't affect the outcome. If you have an external locus of control, spending more time with positive people who believe they will succeed can be helpful; it will help you learn how to take more responsibility for what happens.

Turning things around

When we take a negative mindset, we can begin to believe the negative comments we tell ourselves and this can affect subsequent action. So, because we don't think we will get a job, we don't put enough effort into an application form, we don't do enough research and don't prepare for interviews.

So a change of mindset, to focus more on positive thoughts and also positive behaviours is going to greatly increase our chance of success. It helps us to be more willing to try out new ideas.

IN A NUTSHELL

- What we believe will affect our outcomes; we need to believe we can be successful.
- It's not positive thoughts alone that we need, but thoughts based on evidence of why we should get the job.
- Using positive affirmations will help us to be successful.
- We must believe we are in control and responsible for what happens.
- We must change what we are doing if we don't get the outcome we want.

BEFORE YOU MOVE ON

■ Make a note of three key points
you have learnt.

■ Make a note of what is the top
takeaway, for you, from this
chapter.

3 WHAT AM I GOING TO DO?

You must be clear on your goal – the job you are looking for. Now we'll focus on what you want to do, and, if you work at the moment, why you want to make a change.

You will consider what you could do, what you would like to do, the options available, and then decide – where do you stand the greatest chance of success?

By the end of this chapter you will be able to answer the following questions.

- What do I want to do? What job titles are used?

- What industries do I want to work in?

- Which specific companies/organisations interest me?

The best way to get a new job is to **be very clear on what you want to do.** Be too vague and you aren't fully focused on anything. Having a clear idea of the job you want means that every aspect of your job search is focused on achieving your objective.

This could be something similar to what you have done before, or you may be looking to make a more dramatic change. It is possible to move to something new but if you are looking for a job quickly, the more it fits in with what you have done before the easier it is likely to be.

You need to identify a job/work that will excite you but that is also one where you are likely to be successful, otherwise you are setting yourself up to fail. Your decision may involve reskilling or more extensive retraining. Can you afford to do this or do you need some way of generating an income as you train?

Unless you know what you are looking for, how can anyone help you? Everything you include in your CV and letter must be focused on the job you want.

Being clear on your job-search goal

- Simon lost his job as a driver. He's been a driver for over 30 years. It's what he does and what he's good at, with an unblemished record. He wants another driving job.
- Kevin has been made redundant as a senior sales consultant at a car dealership. He's got an excellent track record and is looking for a similar role.
- Anita worked as a legal executive. She needs another job as she plans to move more than 150 miles to be closer to her daughter following the death of her husband.
- Nilesh wanted to stay within the finance field after redundancy. He knows that his 15-year track record would appeal to other companies.
- Katy was generating little income through her life-coaching business but loved to write. She took an intensive journalism course and now makes a reasonable income through writing.
- Rachael seeks work, and has a range of skills including excellent people skills. Whilst she isn't clear on what she wants, she does get shortlisted and

receives job offers, but she lacks confidence and is still applying for, and being successful in low-level jobs. She could do far more.

■ Gary wanted to keep his options open and applied for everything he thought he could do, but his CV was vague, he couldn't be specific when telling others what he wanted and nine months on is despondent. He's made hundreds of applications and got one interview – just one. Clearly, whatever he was doing wasn't working. I wanted to find out what job he was looking for, as the clearer our focus the easier it is to get the job. He was vague, and that's one of the reasons for his current situation. There's more going wrong, and I'm going to share more of Gary's story throughout this book.

Many people seek to keep their options open but as Gary found, this can make it harder to create a clear message, whether you are talking to somebody or revising your CV. It also means you are going to find it hard to do sufficient research – you can't look in depth if you are focused on too many options.

You won't be successful through trying to keep your options open – the hiring manager or consultant who skims your CV wants to immediately know how you match up to the vacancy. Your CV has to be clear on what you want, and in the next chapter we will go deeper as to why you should get the job. But before we move on …

Do you know what you want to do?
If you can say **yes**, move straight on to the next chapter.

If you are not sure, let's talk you through an approach to give you clarity. You can't get a job till you know what you want. It's not down to a recruitment agency or HR department to work out what it is you should be doing.

Why do I want a new job?

Not everyone who can benefit from this book is unemployed – you could be like Anita, and want to move location for family reasons, or like Richard, and want a change of career and be willing to take the time to make the right choice. When I worked with Richard we focused on what he could do based on his knowledge, skills and abilities alongside understanding his values and drivers and his longer-term vision, but we also covered why he wanted to change jobs.

Richard had become disillusioned with the financial sector. The focus on profit jarred with his values, and the long hours were a killer as he had young children from his second marriage. For Richard, it is less about the money – he has good savings and a mortgage-free home. What is of most importance to him is job satisfaction. When Sue was married it was less important that she only brought in about £15,000 a year as a self-employed consultant, but with a recent divorce she now needs to focus more on generating an income. She says that she wants to return to salaried work.

In most cases it's worth taking time to think about what you don't like about your job and to see if there are things that can be addressed in the short term. If it's the long travel to work, could you work from home a couple of days a week? Could you talk to your boss about how you would prefer to be managed? Could you just say no and start going home at 6 p.m. at least twice a week rather than still being there at 7.30 p.m. most nights?

If you want a bigger challenge, could it be possible within your job – could you take on extra responsibility? Does your boss know how you feel? Sometimes people make assumptions – your boss may be assuming you are winding down towards retirement. If you are still keen to develop and learn, let them know.

What could I do?

When you need a job quickly, review your CV and choose a job to apply for based on what you have done before. Look at your career history and make a note of the one or more jobs that are easily spotted from your CV – probably your current or previous job. Anita wants a new job doing the same, and Nilesh aims for something in a similar field but perhaps slightly different – from management accountant to school business manager. Both should find it easier to get a similar job than to move to something new.

Ask yourself – do these appeal to me?
If one of these is OK and you need to find work quickly, focus on gaining a job and once settled you can take time to explore what you really want to do and plan a move to achieve your new goal. Some research now can still be useful as e.g. working as a marketing manager in a manufacturing environment will be very different to working as a marketing manager in a hotel. But even in the hotel field the role may differ greatly depending on whether it is a large chain

or a small boutique hotel, and if the hotel is based in a large city, for example, or part of an outdoor training company, this will also affect aspects of the job.

What do my skills suggest?

Technical skills may be specific to your job, such as market research, Six Sigma, and database management. There are also skills that are transferable across jobs, such as written communication, team working and commercial awareness. Developing specific skills such as database management or effective use of social media can make us desirable to employers. If these are skills that few people use well, they can help you to stand out.

New skills can also be acquired. Think of senior managers from 15 or so years ago who had a secretary print out emails and then drafted replies. They had to learn keyboard skills. What they saw as a low-level skill became an essential requirement. I've also worked with a marketing director who never became professionally qualified; all was fine till he lost his job at 52. He then found that membership of the Chartered Institute of Management was essential for senior roles.

Look at the skills that underpin your jobs, if you took these apart could they be put together in a different way? The next activity will help to identify your range of skills.

By 50+ we will have amassed a great number of skills, and so in the activity immediately after that I want you to differentiate between them. In particular, which skills do you love and want to use, and which are you good at but sap all your energy – your 'burnout' skills?

The purpose of these exercises is to help you to identify the skills that you want to use in your next job. I could provide a list of literally hundreds of individual skills, but I've opted for this approach, grouping skills into categories. The visual image of your results helps you to 'eyeball' which sets of skills you are most likely to want to use. You can also include any additional skills you would like to use.

SKILL RANKING

Go through each of the skill areas and rank each of the indicators on a 1–3 scale using a X.

1	2	3
None/Low	Moderate	Very high/Expert

Think through all aspects of your life to identify when you have used the different skill: previous jobs, current work and out-of-work interests.

Either complete as you go, or later go back and add YES against each skill that you want to use.

Communication skills	1	2	3		Want to use
Talking fluently and clearly, easy to understand					
Strong listening skills, with accurate recall of what has been said					
Giving instructions					
Explaining difficult ideas or concepts					
Presenting to a group					
Speaking on the phone without misunderstandings					
Reading efficiently and quickly for facts					
Clear writing skills, matched to the purpose					
Logical writing style					
Broad vocabulary					
Can spell with good use of grammar					
Translating complex material into everyday language					
Interpersonal skills	**1**	**2**	**3**		**Want to use**
Getting on well with a range of people					
Working well as part of a team					
Resolving disagreements and dealing with conflict					
Seen as helpful to others					

	1	2	3		Want to use
Dealing effectively with 'difficult people'					
Encouraging people to be open and honest with me					
Willing to apologise when in the wrong					
Demonstrating empathy					
Encouraging others to speak up					
Sensitivity to the feelings and needs of others					
Taking time to help people with personal problems					
Interviewing or assessing people					
Persuading and influencing others					
Being assertive rather than aggressive					
Helping other people to reach their potential					
Selling products and ideas to others					
Giving constructive feedback to others					
Motivating and encouraging others					
Giving helpful and encouraging feedback					
Leadership skills	**1**	**2**	**3**		**Want to use**
Motivating people to work together					
Taking difficult decisions					
Delegating work					
Dealing with problems and crises					
Supervising and/or managing people					
Will value and respect others					
Coaching other people					
Chairing meetings					
Weighing up pros and cons effectively					
Sizing up a situation or person quickly and accurately					
Ability to convey a sense of purpose					
Promoting change and making change happen					

Problem-solving skills	1	2	3		Want to us
Accurately identifying and diagnosing problems					
Getting to the root of a problem, rejecting irrelevant information					
Collecting and integrating data from different sources					
Researching alternative solutions					
Seeing the big picture when solving problems					
Financial and numerical skills	**1**	**2**	**3**		**Want to use**
Remembering numbers – number plates, phone, etc.					
Budgeting well and managing money					
Preparing a budget					
Creating a spreadsheet using Excel					
Familiarity with VAT and taxation					
Producing a cash-flow forecast					
Producing annual accounts					
Carrying out a cost-benefit analysis					
Interpreting management accounts					
Familiarity with operating costing systems					
Understanding different types/sources of loan finance					
Mental arithmetic					
Working out percentages					
Organisational/Planning skills	**1**	**2**	**3**		**Want to use**
Meeting deadlines					
Prioritising, taking account of all relevant information					
Multitasking					
Planning and organising an event					
Working with systems and procedures					
Monitoring of progress					

	1	2	3		
Having a well-organised workspace and filing systems					
Ability to rationalise activities					
Coordinating activities					
Anticipating problems and developing solutions					
Setting achievable objectives and deadlines					
Allocating responsibilities					
Analytical skills	**1**	**2**	**3**		**Want to use**
Analysing information					
Researching and gathering information					
Ability to reach clear conclusions and make sound decisions					
Analysing sales figures					
Understanding profit and loss accounts					
Drawing up a business plan					
Creative/Innovative skills	**1**	**2**	**3**		**Want to use**
Ability to generate alternative solutions to problems					
Good source of creative ideas					
Adapting the ideas of others and applying them in new ways					
Ability to be intuitive or imaginative					
Writing in a creative way					
Ability to see new possibilities					
Using a strong sense of intuition					
Ability to think laterally					
Cooking and creating meals					
Playing and composing music					
Working creatively with colour					
Practical skills	**1**	**2**	**3**		**Want to use**
Manual dexterity skills (hand-eye coordination)					
Using tools and equipment					

	1	2	3		
Diagnosing mechanical and electrical faults					
Constructing or assembling materials or equipment					
Dealing with tangible practical problems					
Working with my hands					
Repairing or restoring things					
Creating scale models					
Driving					
Handling things with precision and speed					
Technical skills	**1**	**2**	**3**		**Want to use**
Understanding recent technical developments					
Using laboratory equipment					
Understanding engineering					
Maintaining or repairing complex equipment					
Using technical equipment					
Learning a new language easily					
Using IT					
Knowledge of social media					

Review your answers and strike through any skills that you don't enjoy using; you don't want to prioritise these for your future career choices.

MOTIVATED AND BURNOUT SKILLS

To identify your motivated and burnout skills, complete the following table.

Motivated v. burnout skills

	VERY PROFICIENT	LESS PROFICIENT
LOVE using these skills	These are your motivated skills	These skills are potential areas for career development
DISLIKE using these skills	These are your burnout skills	

Motivated skills are the skills you are good at and enjoy using; they usually lead to career satisfaction, and you should focus on using these.

Burnout skills are skills you are good at doing, but really don't like to use and so should avoid them in the future.

As you review job sites you will see that your skills and experience do not mean you have to continue in your most recent line of work. For example, skills and experience in healthcare and helping people do not necessarily mean that you need to continue as a nurse. If you were to include organisational and coordination skills alongside being creative, for example, you might be able to seek a move to be a practice manager at a medical practice or a colon hydro-therapist (and plenty of less-dramatic options).

This exercise helped Nilesh to identify school business manager as a suitable job and reminded Phil how much he enjoyed his previous work as an operations manager.

What would I like to do?

This may be your time to make sure you are making the right choice for the next phase of your life, which could easily be another 15 years or more.

Many job-seekers will get support from a career coach – I help many clients to identify their strengths, abilities and clarify a career direction. But you can also utilise career sites to read up more on jobs. The National Careers Service is a good place to start and you can read job profiles through this link – http://bit.ly/ NatCS. For example, there are 40 jobs under the financial services section.

As you identify a job that interests you, you can read up more on the requirements, salary, the skills, interests and qualities required, and find similar jobs. Valerie identified insurance claims handling as a new area she was likely to enjoy and from this site identified that the following skills were required:

- excellent spoken and written communication skills
- tact and assertiveness when dealing with customers
- accuracy and attention to detail
- the ability to work well under pressure
- a professional attitude
- good administrative and computer keyboard skills
- respect for confidential information.

Many of us could provide examples against these headings and we can then use this to adapt our CV and to strengthen our applications. Valerie used this to create a skills-based CV. More on this in Chapter 8, 21st-century CVs.

You may want a more radical change. You've already read how Katy trained in journalism alongside working in her current area. This could work for you, as could taking on a job that is part way between your current job and where you want to go. So, if you are unhappy in marketing but want to work as a fundraiser for a charity, a move to do marketing in a charity could then lead on to an internal change of job. You would be able to demonstrate a strong knowledge of the industry which would support your application.

If you really want to look deeper at your options you will want to spend more time in career discovery, looking at skills and interests, personality and more. This is outside the scope of this book, and a great resource to help you is Corinne Mills' *Career Coach: Your personal workbook for a better career,* or to choose a career coach. You can read more on my services at www. amazingpeople.co.uk.

Before making a decision for a radical move you will want to talk with people and find out more about the pros and cons of each job. Chapter 7, Connecting with others will be helpful. So too will research using LinkedIn, see Chapter 9.

Professional Advice

As a fifty-something person you should be prepared to learn new skills. In my case, nursing skills. I had to do a two-year course in nursing. Time well spent, in that jobs come my way all the time now.

Christopher D. King, CNWL NHS Trust

George was a postman for 35 years, but with some health issues he left at 60 with a small pension. Continuing to earn an income was essential, but he was unsure what he could do; he felt he had nothing to offer. In his spare time George had spent over 20 years talking to the public as part of a living history group, with an in-depth knowledge of medieval history and also a passion for history in general. He gave strong examples of when he spent a week talking with schoolchildren. We then revised his CV to include much more detail from his hobby and this led on to a part-time role at a museum working with the school's outreach section.

Wendy had been a full-time carer to her father for the past eight years. When she last worked she was a secretary and since then had minimal use of a computer so her keyboard skills were rusty. She considered a number of possibilities, and decided to focus on gaining computer skills alongside some voluntary work to build her confidence. Recently she was successful in her application to work as administrator/secretary in a small charity.

YOU'RE HIRED! FIND WORK AT 50+

Jay was over 50 when he retrained as an electrician. He is now working at his local college of higher education.

Whatever new role you are considering, carefully look at the requirements of the job to make sure that you match up and that you will be a credible candidate.

In what industry would I like to work?

There's one other element of preparation and that is to be clear on where you ideally want to work. Are you clear on the industry, company, function, location? You may think you should keep this open but it's also best to have an ideal to aim for.

In many cases, we can do a particular job working in several different industries. A good number of people unhappy in a profession found that

INDUSTRY CHOICES

Look at this list (it's not definitive but to give you an idea of scope) and make a note of the type of industries you want to work with. Seeing this list can help you see the breadth of places to find work.

Agriculture	Elderly	Literacy	Space
Animal Care	Energy	Management	exploration
Animal	Entertainment	Media	Spirituality
protection	Environment	Military	Sports
Art	Family issues	News	Substance
Biotech	Fashion	Non-profit	abusers
Books	Finance	agencies	The homeless
Broadcasting	Food	Nutrition	The sick and
Business	Gardening	Parks and	disabled
Child protection	Government	recreation	The performing
Children	Healthcare	Politics	arts
Churches	Home	Printing and	Technology
Community	healthcare	publishing	Tourism
development	Human	Public safety	Transport
Construction	development	Religion	Travel
Design	Journalism	Research	Youth
Education	Justice/law	Sexuality issues	

moving from, for example, being an accountant in an engineering company to a similar job but in an arts-based organisation, when they have a real passion for arts, lead to increased satisfaction and they kept to a similar income level.

For others it might be that they want to work within, for example, community development but need to find out what options there are.

From this activity Pat found three industries that interested him.

Make a note of ideal organisations, and consider small companies as well. Don't forget to consider location. Are you willing to spend over two hours on travel each day? Be clear now so you don't waste time on applying for the wrong jobs.

Salary

Alongside thinking about what you want, you also need to be flexible over the salary. You may not get a job on the same salary, but you can negotiate – perhaps to work four days for the same salary and be measured on deliverables, not time at your desk. You could also negotiate for flexitime, additional holidays or to work part-time from home.

What are the growth areas? Labour market information (LMI)

A good way of making a choice is to get an understanding of what is happening 'out there' and finding out about the needs of employers, skills required and new jobs that are being created. You will want to understand where there will be growth, and to look at trends.

You can usually find up-to-date information via the National Careers Service – www.nationalcareersservice.direct.gov.uk. Check on availability in your area. For example, if you are seeking work in the Midlands this website will help – www.futuresadvice.co.uk/lmi.html. If you are based in Northern Ireland there's an excellent site – www.nidirect.gov.uk/job-trends.

To help you make a choice over which industry to target, these questions will help. Think of the job you seek.

■ What are the general trends in the industry, by sector?
■ Where are the hotspots – those areas where growth will remain steady for several years? This could be geographic area or a type of product or service.

■ Is this an industry experiencing growth or in decline and are jobs being created in the UK or overseas?

Use your research skills to find out more. You will find helpful guidance in Chapter 11, Taking a direct approach and Chapter 12, Traditional job search.

It's worth looking at up-and-coming jobs – look for areas of growth and to see if you can match with any. Don't forget that every new industry also needs support staff. So if an area interests you, you can demonstrate strong passion through your interest in and knowledge of an area such as biofuels to bolster an application for a support position, or to contact the company direct with a targeted approach.

A government document with lots of ideas for new careers is *Careers of the future*, published in December 2014; find your copy here – www.gov.uk/government/publications/careers-of-the-future. You will find details of more useful links in Appendix 2.

Certain areas are projected to grow much faster than average (employment increase of 22% or more) with increased growth into the year 2022 in careers such as:

■ cardiovascular technologists and technicians
■ actuaries
■ market-research analysts and marketing specialists
■ genetic counsellors
■ allergists and immunologists
■ biofuel engineers and processing technicians
■ distance-learning coordinators
■ neuropsychologists.

So, whilst you may not be qualified to become a biofuel engineer, you could explore the biofuel industry, identify organisations and approach them for roles working in finance, operations, purchasing, etc.

Far better to approach organisations working in these areas than, for example, travel agents, where there is little likelihood of growth.

> **Case Study**
>
> Pat said: 'It was interesting to see "distance learning coordinator" there as I did distance-tutoring for 10 years, but Gloucestershire University closed that degree. Also, I enjoyed online tutoring for the OU but the online-only short courses stopped using tutors, and other courses required travel to tutorial centres, which in the southwest region are far-flung … maybe I should look around for other employers of distance tutors?'

Retraining

It's worth finding out what training is available to move into new areas. Talk with the staff at your local job centre (if unemployed) or talk to an advisor with the National Careers Service to find out about options.

This could include taking on an apprenticeship. Over the past five years the number of over-50s taking these has risen from 400 to 2,480 – about 10% of all apprentices. You could also be proactive and seek an internship, similar to what recent graduates do. Dr Ros Altmann, the government's older workers' champion, promotes 'returnships' and there have been examples in the press of employers saying that they welcome training older people who tend to stay with the same employer for longer than younger ones. Barclays is just one organisation to encourage older people onto apprenticeship schemes.

> **Case Study**
>
> Lauren returned to the workplace after two years caring for her father. She found a job working in admin for a care home, and was able to complete an apprenticeship in business administration alongside it, giving her confidence in her abilities. This helped her progress within her career.
>
> Bob became a joiner's apprentice in his late forties. Whilst recognising the money was poor, it led on to a new direction and he now works with his son, fitting bedroom units.
>
> Pat is currently doing a fully paid internship in IT support. He said that the other interns are all much younger. He said, 'A week before the interview leading to my present job, I had a phone interview for an internship as a social-media intern for an NGO, which I was offered but then found it was

unpaid, and that wasn't viable for me. I thought I would be good at that because I knew tools for response analysis and reporting, and also I can assess the quality of information sources and avoid some of the blunders that may give visitors a bad impression.'

If you are good with numbers, retraining in accountancy/bookkeeping is well known as a good way to get into a new job. Peter took part-time qualifications, starting at 57, and by 61 had his own accountancy practice. William also retrained in accountancy and got a new job as an accountant aged 64 and is still there at 71.

If you are considering something new, you may want to think of working in a call centre. The call-centre industry has generally employed young members of staff and also has a high turnover. Many employers are now appreciating how older members of staff are far more likely to stay. At our age many of us can empathise with customer concerns, and our approach can also be motivational for younger members of staff. Some, such as Domestic and General, are proactive in recruiting older staff, recognising our experience, loyalty and reliability. They also have induction training to include building confidence, and offer flexible working.

Are you a credible applicant?

This chapter has got you looking at what you could do, and what your skills suggest, alongside checking out that this is an area of growth.

Before you move on, make sure that you will be a credible candidate. Much as you may want to make a radical career change, are you likely to get the job? Look at the requirements, make sure you have the relevant experience, and you are more likely to be successful.

Case Study

Suzanne said: 'Since I left my job last month, apart from taking some time out and generally not rushing around, I've started focusing on two main areas. The first is sorting out my CV and starting to look for jobs like the one I left, teaching English as a foreign language. The second is exploring alternative ways to earn money in addition to teaching in a language school.'

We'll explore more on this second option in Chapter 13.

I want you to be clear on the job and industry so you can target your CV. Whilst I want you to focus on just one job, you could choose two … if one of them is to do something closely related to what you have done before alongside a plan to move into a new area – like Katy and journalism/writing.

CLARITY

Make sure you can answer these questions.

- What do I want to do? What job titles are used?
- What industries do I want to work in?

- Are there specific companies/ organisations that interest me? Write them down.

I appreciate this can be hard. Pat said that he tried out a variety of ways to help him to identify this, including fasting for 3 days, but never got any inspiration. The more practical suggestions within this chapter should help you, and Pat now has more than one job that interests him.

Once you have reached a decision you can review and revise your CV, but there's a step to work through before that, to be clear on why you should get the job. This is covered in the next chapter.

IN A NUTSHELL

This chapter has focused on getting you clear on the job you want. It might not be your dream job, and it may be a step back, but it's a job where you are likely to be successful.

You are also clear on the industries that you want to work in, with some dream employers also identified.

BEFORE YOU MOVE ON

- Make a note of three key points you have learnt.
- Make a note of what is the top takeaway, for you, from this chapter.

- **Write down what job you are looking for.**

4 WHY SHOULD I GET THE JOB?

You are now clear on the job you are going to apply for. The focus of this chapter is **why**. You need to be clear:

■ why you should get the job ahead of everyone

■ who you are and what makes you valuable

■ why you need a value proposition, and by the end of this chapter you will have created one.

B y now you know the job you want and have a target industry. This chapter is very practical, so work your way through the stages.

Nilesh is seeking employment as a school business manager, Phil as an operations manager and Anita to continue as a legal executive. In the end they all got a job faster than Gary and Sue, who struggled, partly due to being unclear on what they wanted to do. As they continued to be unsuccessful in their job search they eventually made a decision on what to apply for, but their job search took months longer than if they had been clear at the beginning.

At 50+ we may face (hidden) discrimination, so we need to make an excellent application. We must demonstrate **how** we are valuable to an organisation and **why** we should get the job. First, so we get shortlisted and later, so we can win through at interview. In a later chapter, I will discuss making direct approaches to organisations, again it is essential you are clear on the value you offer – why they should want to employ you.

Why should an employer choose you?

It's essential to understand why any employer would want to offer you the job. What can you offer that differentiates you from others applying for the same job? It could be knowledge, experience, personality, something outside of work, your work ethic . . . you need to know why you. What do you have to offer?

I advise you to make sure you complete the activity below before moving on to revise your CV, applying for jobs, etc., as this is one of the key foundation steps you need to complete.

ACTIVITY 12

THE JOB I WANT

I am clear on the job I'm going to apply for.

You worked on this in the previous chapter. Write it down, nice and clear so you don't get distracted by shiny job ads that tempt you away.

The job is _____

The relevant experience I have is

_____

_____

_____

_____

_____

My signature skills, the top four to five things I'm really good at are

1. _____

2. _____

3. _____

4. _____

5. _____

We need to understand what makes us different from others who will be vying for the same job. This may be how we approach a task or how we have dealt with challenges. Why should we get the job?

If you are stuck, review job ads and make a note of the skills listed and see the ones you have. Use the National Careers Service website and job boards to get more detail. **Do complete this task before you move on.**

Are you clear on your experience and skills that are relevant to the job you seek? Understanding our top skills and being clear on relevant experience is a great start, but many others will share our skills and experience so what else can we offer? We'll cover that shortly.

Personality – I understand who I am

We are all different. No-one else has our unique blend of skills, experience and personality traits, and we need to focus on these positive qualities, not our age. Personality is an important aspect of this.

Does your personality make you want to spend time with people, prefer to be in the background, be creative or more detail-orientated? This next activity will help you identify key aspects of your personality.

CHOOSE DESCRIPTIVE WORDS

Go through this list and put a tick by the words that describe you, then shortlist further using two ticks. You should aim for a list of seven to 10 top descriptive words.

Then take time to write down a description of what, for example, being 'curious' means to you. Then do the same for 'supportive', etc.

Abstract thinker	Astute	Cool	Disdainful
Academic	Authoritative	Co-operative	Dismayed
Accepting	Bashful	Courageous	Disorganised
Accurate	Boring	Crazy	Dominant
Achievement-	Broad-minded	Creative	Down-to-earth
driven	Businesslike	Credible	Dynamic
Action-orientated	Calm	Curious	Easy-going
Adaptable	Carefree	Customer-	Efficient
Adventurous	Careful	focused	Effective
Affectionate	Caring	Daring	Emotional
Afraid	Cautious	Decisive	Empathic
Aggressive	Changeable	Defeated	Energetic
Aggrieved	Charismatic	Deferential	Enterprising
Aloof	Cheated	Defiant	Enthusiastic
Ambitious	Cold	Deliberate	Exceptional
Amused	Commercially	Dependable	Exciting
Analytical	aware	Dependent	Expedient
Angry	Committed	Depressed	Experienced
Annoyed	Competent	Detail-orientated	Expert
Anxious	Competitive	Determined	Firm
Appreciative	Confident	Diligent	Flexible
Apprehensive	Confused	Diplomatic	Focused
Articulate	Conservative	Disappointed	Foolish
Ashamed	Consistent	Disciplined	Forgiving
Assertive	Content	Discreet	Forthright

Friendly	Loyal	Rejected	Suspicious
Frustrated	Matter-of-fact	Reliable	Sympathetic
Fun-loving	Mature	Relieved	Tactful
Generous	Methodical	Remorseful	Take initiative
Gentle	Mild	Resentful	Talented
Gloomy	Mischievous	Reserved	Talkative
Grateful	Modest	Resilient	Task-orientated
Grounded	Motivated	Resourceful	Team builder
Guarded	Objective	Responsible	Team player
Happy	Open	Responsive	Tenacious
Helpful	Orderly	Risk-taker	Tender
Helpless	Organised	Sad	Tense
Hostile	Outgoing	Satisfied	Tetchy
Humiliated	Outstanding	Sceptical	Theoretical
Humorous	Over-sensitive	Scornful	Thick-skinned
Hysterical	Panicky	Self-assured	Thin-skinned
Idealistic	Patient	Self-controlled	Thorough
Imaginative	Peeved	Self-critical	Tidy
Impatient	Penetrating	Self-motivated	Timid
Impulsive	Perceptive	Self-reliant	Tolerant
Indecisive	Persevering	Self-righteous	Traditional
Independent	Persistent	Sensitive	Trapped
Indifferent	Persuasive	Serene	Triumphant
Individualistic	Pioneering	Serious	Trusting
Industrious	Pleased	Shy	Unassuming
Influential	Positive	Silly	Understanding
Innovative	Practical	Sincere	Unique
Insightful	Pragmatic	Slow	Unsettled
Intellectual	Precise	Sociable	Unusual
Introspective	Predictable	Sophisticated	Vengeful
Jealous	Private	Sorrowful	Versatile
Joyful	Proactive	Sorry	Vicious
Judgemental	Protective	Spontaneous	Vigorous
Kind	Proud	Steady	Visionary
Knowledgeable	Punctual	Stimulating	Warm
Lacking ambition	Questioning	Straightforward	Wary
Light-headed	Quick	Strategic thinker	Weak
Literate	Quiet	Strong	Wilful
Lively	Rational	Successful	Witty
Logical	Reactive	Sulky	Worrier
Lost	Realistic	Supportive	
Loving	Reflective	Surprised	

Some words you may want to tick, but if they aren't a descriptor of you, resist. You have to be able to back up these qualities with practical examples.

Case Study

Pat said: 'I found nine words to describe me just going through the As and suggested to Denise that I should limit myself to two from each letter. She explained that I may well start with a very big list but then to narrow down and narrow down to get to the top 10 or 15. Grouping words together helped too, such as "creative and innovative" and also "consistent and dependable".'

An alternative approach is to search online for a free personality assessment. These will never be as helpful as spending time with a career psychologist but you can get an overview. Probably the best option is to look up the Big Five personality test. There are many available, such as http://personality-testing.info/tests/BIG5.php.

The best way to get a job is to be authentic about who you are. Don't pretend to be someone else. If you are thoughtful, measured and quiet, look for where this will be a bonus, for example a role where you communicate online rather than attending too many meetings.

Professional qualities

It may be our professional values that help us to stand out from younger applicants. How well can you demonstrate the following qualities?

- **Motivation and energy** – Are you self-motivated? Are you eager to learn? Do you put in the extra effort to achieve a goal?
- **Commitment and reliability** – Are you dedicated to your profession? Willing to go beyond the job description? Are you engaged in your own career management? Do you deliver what you promise?
- **Determination** – Do you have the drive and determination to get things done? The resilience to bounce back?
- **Pride and integrity** – Are you committed to doing your best? Do you take responsibility for your actions, even when things go wrong?
- **Productivity** – Do you make good use of your time and resources?

Can you say yes to all of these or some of them? You may like to use some of these as key words in your LinkedIn profile and CV but you must have examples to back these up.

What makes you uniquely valuable to potential employers?

Discover your hook – what is special about you?
What skills and accomplishments set you apart from every other person who does the work you seek? It's not easy to determine what makes us special and unique, but it's important to think about it if you are going to market yourself. Think about your work. What do you accomplish better than anyone else? (Or, better than most people?) Have you been able to solve a problem and come up with solutions no-one else could? Think about the results you create; how do you make a difference? **If you don't know what makes you distinct, it will be difficult to convince anyone else why they should hire you.**

ACTIVITY 14

MY GOOD QUALITIES

Start making a list of each and every thing you do that's a little bit better than others. Also, ask people. Sometimes other people have a better perspective on what we have to offer. Rachael has a varied work history and felt that she had nothing special to offer, but talking with friends and new work colleagues helped her realise she could do far more than what she had applied for in the past.

This is not the time to be modest and shy, so over the next few days keep adding to your list.

Understanding this will be helpful at interview but you also need to understand this right at the start of your application. You need to be able to answer the question why an employer should choose you.

There are many ways that we are the same – education, work experience, way of working, being organised and/or creative, etc. Rather than focus on all the ways we are the same, it's better to focus on how we are different. Maybe you have some special experience that you can call on, or you do a task in a different way, or your passion and enthusiasm shine through all you do.

SAME AND DIFFERENT

Think about other people who do similar work to what you seek, perhaps a couple of colleagues either now or in the past. List the skills you share in common, and perhaps your education, but also focus on how you are different. You can start making a note now and add to it.

Clearly there will be many other people who also want to do the job you seek, so you need to be crystal clear – not woolly and vague – as to why an employer should offer you the job. Anita can say that she is a legal executive and that she has good customer-service skills but this doesn't focus on the specific benefit that she can bring. You will see in Chapter 8, 21st-century CVs, how just a few words can convey the value she offers.

We will cover connecting with others in Chapter 7. The benefits of meeting other people who work in your area is that by comparing yourself to them – whether they be project managers, store managers or fundraisers – you are able to see the ways you stand out.

Who do you want to work for?
I'd like you to think about the organisation you want to work for.

What experience will they be most interested in?

How will they benefit from recruiting you? Will you help them to:

- earn more money?
- handle their work more efficiently to save money?
- attract more customers?
- solve some problem?
- create a new product or service?

How do you differ from other people who are also interested in the same job?

CREATE EXAMPLES

Go beyond just reading this, and write down examples that you can refer to again.

As noted earlier, some industries are more likely to grow, so review the industries on offer and aim for growth areas such as home healthcare, and pharmacy, rather than travel agents, for example.

Once you have a list, do due diligence to see if you want to work in that field. You can find out more from talking to people who work there and former employees; again, use LinkedIn to help you. This will help you create your highly targeted letter.

Some organisations are noted for employing younger workers. Online salary information company PayScale looked at the age of workers at 32 top tech companies; 25% had a median age of employees of 30 or younger. Firms that are growing tend to have younger workers but organisations can benefit from our maturity and experience – organisations don't work as well when everyone is the same. So, **we need to emphasise how we can add value.**

Alongside a focus on the organisations, I'd also like you to consider who are the influential players in the field and how can you get to know them. Look them up on LinkedIn and identify the groups they belong to. Do you know anyone who can make the connection?

Adding value
I'd like you to think about how you add value to an organisation. There's probably lots you can say but what would be the stand-out elements? For me, as a career psychologist, it is about keeping at the forefront and sharing knowledge, creative ideas and prompt responses.

With Rachael, it is her ability to listen and relationship-building skills. She said, 'I got the job because I was prepared to listen. I had the same qualification as others; it wasn't because I could do the job better. They offered me the job because they liked me.'

With Kevin, it was his knowledge and contacts. He had a contacts list of so many people who he'd sold cars to in the past and kept in touch with, many through his leisure and charity interests.

Professional Advice

There is a great temptation to knock 15 years off your age just to get an interview! The fact that I had pushed hard and obtained an MBA from the OU did not really open doors in new career areas given my age. The steady drip, drip of rejection letters does eventually start to shake your confidence. I decided to market myself as a consultant in my previous work area and that did pay dividends, showing that if you stick to what you know well, and leverage all your old contacts, it can pay dividends. Twelve years on I am still working flat out, which is really great, and my MBA on the CV I am sure does no harm now. An MBA seems to be the added value that all managers need, as well as their technical expertise and associated degree these days, so all that hard work did pay off.

John Bennett, Hydrographic Survey Consultant,
BennCo2 Ltd

Your value proposition

In business jargon, a value proposition is a summary of why a consumer should buy a particular product or service over another. Value propositions are used as part of the job-search process, but most people don't bother, so this is one way to get you ahead of the rest.

Ask yourself, if you were competing against ten other people with similar experience and qualifications, why would a company want to hire *you* over *them*? What's special about you? The work you have already done in this chapter will help you to answer this question.

This can include your age – how can you make this a real bonus to a new employer? Is it your depth of knowledge, the way you have dealt with significant setbacks, the contacts you have?

FIRST DRAFT VALUE PROPOSITION

Create a first draft value proposition – what is special about you? What is the value you add?

The work that you do in this area has to focus on the job you want, not what went before. Make sure your examples are all focused on your job target.

If you can't answer this question, you will find it hard to refine your CV, cover letter and convince at interview. Your preparation for a new job must include this key statement of the value you add. This focuses on what you will do in the job, not what you have already done, but you can refer to some of your experience.

I encourage my clients to write it down – word for word, as they will often use it in written format. Therefore, you write this in the active voice rather than the past tense. The focus is on what you are going to do next.

Yes, it takes time, but it is helpful because it makes sure that you are clear on:

■ what sets you apart from the competition
■ what you have to offer.

Use this to help market yourself to (persuade) others. For example, a shorter version can be used in your LinkedIn profile and also for when you introduce yourself to others.

Saying 'I am a retail store manager' is just quoting a job description. It has far more impact if you can say something like: 'goal-driven, enthusiastic and motivational store manager'.

WHY SHOULD YOU GET THE JOB?

Can you now answer the question – Why should you get the job?

If it's a definite 'yes', that's excellent.

Is it just in your head or down on paper? I'd like you to write it down as if you were answering the common interview question – why should we give you the job?

If it's a 'maybe', then re-read this chapter and complete all the exercises.

If you are having a problem completing the activity you may want to consider if you are approaching the wrong job. Or perhaps your confidence has been knocked and you are finding it hard to see your strengths. It may be useful to re-read Chapter 2, Mindset.

IN A NUTSHELL

At the start of this chapter you were clear on the job you were going to apply for. This chapter has focused on why you should get the job. The activities you have undertaken have helped you to understand:

- more about who you are – particular aspects of your personality
- your hook – what is special about you
- the type of organisation you want to work for
- why a particular organisation would want to recruit you.

BEFORE YOU MOVE ON

- Make a note of three key points you have learnt.
- Make a note of what is the top takeaway, for you, from this chapter.

- **Ensure you can clearly answer the question 'Why should you get the job?'**

5 PROCESSES AND SYSTEMS

This chapter will help you to work more effectively by sharing tips and practical ideas so that you have simplified processes and you don't end up as a full-time administrator. This will include:

■ managing your time

■ filing systems

■ when to review possible jobs.

It will also provide you with a weekly plan and explain why you need an activity log.

We will look at whether you are able to hold yourself accountable or if you need additional support.

You now know what you want to do and why you should get the job, so let's get you focused on success. You will need to talk with people you know and set up conversations with others; create and review your marketing material – your CV, LinkedIn profile and much more. Whilst most people concentrate on traditional ways of getting a job, I'll explain later why this is least effective and that it is more important to take charge and contact companies direct. You may also want to consider working for yourself.

But first you need to make sure that you have good systems in place to help you to manage your job search.

Managing your time

How much time can you devote to your job search? If you are not in work, your job hunt *can* be your full-time job, but it shouldn't be. Use your time wisely; you don't need to spend more than five hours a day on all aspects of your job search. When you get an interview you need some slack in your diary for preparation, both for doing tasks and also time for mental preparation. If you are working, it's even more important to plan your time; if you have a longish commute, see how much you can do on the train/bus. Be realistic: you can always do more, but have a set amount of time, say 10–15 hours, spread out over the week.

Decide when you will check job ads, write applications, do research, phone people. Also allow time to undertake development activity – learn new skills, read industry-relevant papers and also time for the gym and other personal interests. If you have been made redundant, it's tempting to perhaps take a two-week holiday, then spend a month decorating, but before you know it three months have gone by and very little progress has been made.

Focus

Too many of my clients spend too long on household tasks – decorating, helping out their children and looking after grandchildren. Yes, it's nice to help but if you want a new job, you have to prioritise your job search.

There are plenty of domestic/personal tasks that you would do after work. Do not prioritise these now. Each day you need time to do the following five tasks, and you must prioritise the first two – these should take up well over 50% of your job-search time.

1. Network and build referrals.
2. Contact people and make direct approaches.
3. Review job sites.
4. Make applications.
5. Personal commitments – family, household tasks, etc.

I suggest you keep track of your time and review progress each week. Far too many people focus their time on the bottom of this list. You must focus on the first two. Each evening, make a note of the activity you will do for these first two options on the next day and prioritise it.

Systems and admin

I love systems, they make our lives easier. Job-hunting can take over our lives, and whilst your job search can be seen as a full-time job, it's not meant to mean you become a full-time administrator.

Filing system

You will want to have both online and paper-based filing systems so you can quickly access relevant copies of your CV, etc. You also need to have all your certificates and diplomas ready, as you often need to show these to confirm your qualifications.

Each time you apply for a job, keep a copy of the job ad, the relevant version of your CV and your cover letter so you can refer to them again. Keeping each in a separate plastic wallet could be helpful. Also keep copies of your correspondence each time you make a direct approach to an organisation. I prefer printed copies, and you probably do too.

At times you will have to post a letter or application – not *quite* everything is done online – so have some good quality paper available to use.

Have an online or paper system to schedule tasks (daily and weekly 'to do' lists) and keep track of appointments.

Identify relevant websites
We cover this in Chapter 12, Traditional job search. You can use job aggregators to simplify the process. Set up the alerts with clear parameters so you only get relevant jobs sent to your inbox.

Review possible jobs
You only need to do this once a day. Set aside a period of time, perhaps 30 minutes, to have a coffee and to review the job ads you have been sent. You can then shortlist the ones to apply for.

Many times I hear of people like Gary who apply for 100+ jobs a week. The only way they can do this is to use a generic CV and submit it with a standard cover letter. They then experience rejection again and again.

Stop wasting your time applying for jobs you have no chance of getting and start focusing on jobs where you match the requirements.

Wait until you are interview-ready before you start to apply for jobs. If you 'blow it' with a particular company, it may be harder to be considered for any future jobs that may be on offer.

Home computer and printer
Simon doesn't have a computer or a smartphone, which made his job search, and communicating with me, difficult. He had to rely on the library, and it meant he could not be as responsive to adverts. It makes life much easier if you have regular internet access. Rachael had a laptop but not a printer and she too realised it was more difficult without being able to print paper copies to review.

Your job-search plan
Plan for what you are going to do, set goals for the coming week and keep track of your activity so that you can see the progress you have made. Make a note of who you have spoken with, applications made, etc. Each time you upload your CV keep track of which version and where. This weekly plan should help.

ACTIVITY 20

MY WEEKLY PLAN – W/C:_____

My three key goals are:

1

2

3

Action steps I need to take	Resources needed	Time needed	Due date

You will probably find it helpful to allocate a certain amount of time and to keep to these time commitments. When you set aside 60 or 90 minutes to do something you will get far more done than when you start a task, like reviewing job ads with no clear commitment on the time you will spend.

Include some time each day for something physical – visit the gym, go for a run or a brisk walk out in the fresh air.

Keep an activity log

You may like to create an activity log where you make a note of *everything* you have done, so at the end of each day you can remind yourself of what you did that helped your job-search process and if anything hindered it. This can then help to identify what to do the next day that will have the greatest impact. At the end of each week you can also answer the following questions.

- How many jobs have I applied for which are a close match to what I want?
- How many interviews have I had?
- How many job-search phone calls have I made?
- How much relevant research have I undertaken?
- How many people have I connected with?
- How many people have I reconnected with?
- How many people have I connected with on LinkedIn?
- How many direct approaches have I made?
- How many professional meetings have I attended?

ACTIVITY LOG

Create your own activity log.

At the end of each day make a note of how much time you have spent on each job-search activity (using categories), check how much time you spent on personal tasks and how much time for others. You can then review progress each week.

Case Study

Suzanne said: 'In terms of how I'm spending my time, I'm now becoming stricter about doing work-related activities. It's great being able to get up later, visit people and not rush around, but it's easy for time to pass and I know my redundancy money won't last forever! One thing I'm excited about is finally having time to do a running programme called Couch to 5K. I've wanted to do it for a long time, but couldn't fit it in when I was working full time. It's a very gradual programme and I'm hoping I'll get far enough so I'll be able to continue it when I'm working again.'

Who will hold you accountable?

Think about how you will keep yourself motivated. If you have been looking for a new job for a while is what you are doing working for you, or do you need a job-search buddy or a job-search coach? Someone that you can report to each week to discuss your progress and keep you focused? Perhaps you are strong enough to do this yourself?

Either you or someone else needs to help you stay accountable and set yourself targets, goals and monitor progress.

Finding your next job

Don't fall into the trap of focusing purely on jobs advertised in the press or online. This is the least-effective way of finding a job. Rather than try to 'push' into an organisation through job sites and the ATS system (see Chapter 12), which will always be a struggle, aim to get 'pulled' into an organisation through people you know. People who know the quality of your work and how well you will fit into the organisation.

The best way of finding a job is to use your network and to make direct contact with companies you want to work for. I explain this in much more detail in Chapter 11, Taking a direct approach.

Alongside a focus on the organisations, I'd also like you to consider who the influential players are in the field and how you can get to know them. Look them up on LinkedIn and identify the groups they belong to. Do you know anyone who can make the connection? We'll go into more detail in Chapters 7 and 11.

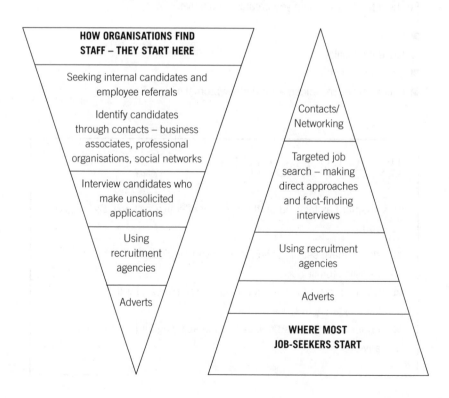

> **Case Study**
>
> Richard found this really helpful and said that it hit home what was going wrong in his job search. He told me he now understood the importance of using marketing techniques. He also was clearer on the need to reconnect with people we know.

Keeping busy

Yes, you will be job-hunting but you also need to do something that keeps you marketable. I've got lots of suggestions in Chapter 13, Alternatives to a permanent full-time job. You could also do voluntary work but make sure this will be something that enhances your CV.

Marketing process

You need to develop marketing material which is focused on the job you want and why you should get the job.

Further chapters will help you create an effective:

- CV
- LinkedIn profile
- direct-approach letter
- online presence, voicemail and other promotional materials.

IN A NUTSHELL

This chapter has focused on the need for effective systems. By now you:

- should have set up a filing system and be clear on which websites to use
- will appreciate the need for a job-search plan and will be keeping an activity log
- understand the need to look beyond applying for jobs that are advertised

- will have considered whether someone else needs to help you by being an accountability partner.

BEFORE YOU MOVE ON

- Make a note of three key points you have learnt.
- Make a note of what is the top takeaway, for you, from this chapter.

- **Have you now got a system in place?**

6 I'M 65+

Whilst the suggestions within the main part of this book are equally relevant to readers aged 65+, I also want to cover some of the issues more relevant to older readers.

Around this time you may be thinking about retirement, so a phased retirement is covered.

It may also be a time for a big adventure – let me share Lyn's story.

Alas, we may begin to attend more funerals; it can be a good reminder to have a wider circle of friends, across the ages.

I f you still feel active and vibrant, then the other chapters will help. But what do we do when we are beginning to feel our age?

As we age things change, our energy levels may decrease, we may have some health issues, but this doesn't mean that we want to give up and retire. We may still want to work – for the social aspect or to mean we have some income; our pension is enough but we'd like a bit extra, too.

Phased retirement

This may be the time to consider a phased retirement. Considering both what we want to do and also making sure that we have enough money for a retirement that could last for 30 years.

Maybe now we need to consider part-time working, a job where we can work just a couple of times a week or, for example, four hours a day.

Maybe it's time for a change – we may need to sit down more, or to opt for a less stressful existence. The thought of serving customers in a call centre is now something that seems right for us. You don't need to be on your feet all day and they welcome older employees who are seen as having better skills in relating to customers.

Are you feeling that you are past it? Is your head full of negative thoughts? Whether you are looking to continue in full-time work or slow down towards retirement, you need to have belief in yourself. Re-reading Chapter 2, Mindset, will help.

As I reach my mid-sixties, I expect to begin to take things easier, to work part-time and to focus on what I want to do: work I enjoy, rather than having to say yes to every opportunity. Other self-employed people I have spoken with have similar expectations.

Time for an adventure

Lyn had been self-employed for many years as a trainer and researcher, and gradually shifted from chasing contracts to undertaking much of her work 'pro bono', being able to focus on what she enjoyed and skip the rest. The opportunity arose to spend most of a year in Italy. Her attitude was that, at 65, you won't get many more chances for adventures. An approach to professional acquaintances in Italy brought the offer of desk-space, and new colleagues to counteract the risk of feeling lonely. Lyn reminded me that language-learning at a mature age is a proven way to stave off Alzheimer's, so it has a health benefit as well.

Cross-generational friendships

Knowing people across generations can also be useful if our friends become ill, perhaps even move into a home, and we lose touch; we want to keep a wider circle of friends to keep us young and to help us have a wider perspective than just talking with people with similar views to us.

Revisit other chapters

Make sure your CV is focused on the needs of the job you seek, and with perhaps nearly 50 years of work history, omit a good chunk of your earlier career history. All the advice in Chapter 8, 21st century CVs, will be relevant to you. You should be able to make a choice of what you want to do, not constrained by income alone. This may be your last job, so what do you want to do? What sort of people do you want to spend time with? How will this fit into other interests such as travel, a hobby and voluntary work?

Help with focus can be found in Chapter 3, but you might be fine just with a job, and happy with a less-demanding job where you turn up, do your job and go. Make sure it's the right thing for you, and you are not settling for something below what you really want.

If you still have bags of energy and plan to stay working for many years to come then of course get focused, and using Chapter 4, Why should I get the job?, will help you be ready to make your case.

Many people can benefit from external support, either from a career coach or from a friend. It may be that you know someone who has followed the path you want, and they may be a helpful role model. If I decide to move overseas in my sixties, I'll certainly be in touch with Lyn.

If you are seeking part-time work in a large retail store then looking at the job details in the store and on their website is probably useful.

Don't forget that not every job or opportunity is advertised. People of different ages have access to different contacts, so you may like to think about the people you know and see that they cross generations. It may be that friends of your children or even grandchildren will hear about a job that is right for you.

At all ages we almost always need to be on LinkedIn, so get over your inhibitions and create a great profile. Chapter 9 contains everything you need.

If you don't think you take a good photo, get it professionally done or get a friend to take lots till you find one you do like. We also need to make sure we can be found and are happy to promote ourselves through an online presence. Whilst it would be good to learn the skills to do this, if you don't already have them, equally you could call on a teenage grandchild to do it for you.

It may be that you need some additional income but not a 'proper job' so consider ways you could generate income such as dog-walking, sewing and alterations, or freelance writing. Chapter 13 covers a good number of ideas for you to consider.

When I talk with older clients they often lack confidence, too much negative self-talk telling them that they are too old, so see Chapter 15 for ways to stay motivated. And don't think you are too old to learn – Chapter 16 has lots of ways to develop yourself. I'm very interested in how physics is used in the kitchen and as I write this have signed up for a free edX course, 'From Haute Cuisine to Soft Matter Science' – read my blog to find out how I got on.

IN A NUTSHELL

This chapter has focused on special advice and suggestions for those at 65+:

- taking a phased-retirement approach.
- considering a 'big adventure'.
- a reminder to have a wider circle of friends, across the ages.

ACTIVITY 23

BEFORE YOU MOVE ON

- Make a note of three key points you have learnt?
- Make a note of what is the top takeaway, for you, from this chapter.

- **Is there anything you would love to do? Can you plan for this?**

7 CONNECTING WITH OTHERS

Research shows that personal connections can result in a higher probability of getting hired.

In this chapter you will learn:

■ about the five types of contact and the need to connect with all groups

■ the importance of connecting with people who are loose connections

■ why you need a ten-second story and not a two-minute elevator speech

■ how to build your tribe

■ the four situations where you need to connect.

This chapter is called 'connecting' rather than 'networking' on purpose. The term networking fills me with dread – too many memories of meetings with everyone trying to sell me something, and desperate job-seekers asking 'Gizza job.' Many introverts, like Richard, Anita and myself find networking very difficult, but when we think of it as having a conversation with one person it is much easier.

Connecting well can lead to a job offer. Not necessarily from the person you talk with but this may be a step to get you 'on the radar' of a decision-maker.

Who we know

The process of hiring 'who you know' can be seen as very discriminatory by people who believe that job offers should be based on what you can do. Some people refuse to reach out to people they don't know but this approach works, so don't ignore it.

Professional Advice

Your next big break will not come from some mysterious technology or discovery of new information. Your next break will come from someone you know.

Derek Sivers,
Founder and Former President of CD Baby

Finding work is increasingly about who you know – your connections telling you about potential opportunities and also giving you the inside scoop on their organisation. As 50+ job-seekers, we have the benefit of a much greater number of connections than younger people, but we also need to make sure that our connections cross generations – younger contacts may have a very different circle of people they know and one of them may know of an opportunity that is perfect for us.

You may read that 60% or more jobs come from networking, but it has to be done well. It isn't asking people directly if they have a job, or know of any vacancies within their company. The chances are they will say no and that's the end of the conversation.

Referrals and social networking are the main ways that companies find new members of staff. The amount invested in finding staff through job boards is in decline. Employers are increasingly seeking referrals, so you need to make sure that you are recommended. Hence the need to reconnect with people from your past.

You must focus much more time and energy on nurturing and leveraging connections rather than applying for jobs. Ideally this is done before you really need help from others.

There are many examples of people getting job offers despite not having applied for the job. For example, meeting someone in a pub, getting on well with a new friend and finding out that they are looking for a new operations manager, and your expertise fits the bill. Just today, a client rang to say she had met up with someone she used to work for and who encouraged her to submit her CV for a job working in her department (the job isn't advertised yet). She's highly likely to get an interview and has a good chance of a job offer. Another client, Julia got to find out about opportunities though contacting other people she knew who worked in this area, but also as she thought more broadly and chatted to a neighbour – the neighbour was ready to make an introduction.

One reason this works is that you know each other through a shared contact, whose opinion the recruiter values.

To be successful you need to have built stronger relationships where people know who you are and what you can do and they can then, possibly, recommend you. Ideally you have nurtured your connections over the years and you aren't just reaching out of the blue and hoping that will be enough. If you haven't, you will need to start with those closer to you and to seek their help.

The people we know fall into five categories.

1. **Close contacts** – we are in touch with these on a regular basis. Our family, friends, and business colleagues we regularly talk with.
2. **Professional colleagues** – people from our professional group that we connect with on an irregular basis.

3. **Online contacts** – we may not meet up but we discuss things online such as in LinkedIn groups. It can also include our Facebook connections.
4. **Casual contacts** – chance encounters, such as people we meet at the gym, at evening class or we get chatting to on the train.
5. **People from the past** – previous colleagues, school friends, neighbours.

Our close contacts are often people like us so it can be more helpful to get in touch with people we don't know as well, those with whom we have a more casual relationship. Rather than try to aim for a dream list of people with the best contacts, get in touch with everyone. We don't know who they know and it's these second-level contacts that are important. At this point you are just sharing an update, see who gets back, exchange an email or two and then perhaps arrange to meet up.

Even if you are an accountant and are seeking another similar role, don't limit your enquiries to people you already know – people working in other fields may get to hear of vacancies in different areas through the people that they know.

Case Study

When sociologist Mark Granovetter did a study of how people got new jobs, he discovered that over half had found their latest job through personal contacts and less than 20% through the traditional route of job ads and recruitment agencies. When he investigated further into the 'personal contacts' he found it was not close friends, but mainly acquaintances.

It's through loose connections or 'weak ties' rather than close friendships that we learn of job opportunities, so getting to know people is an important element of any job search. With the growth of LinkedIn it doesn't have to be face-to-face, although face-to-face is likely to have more value.

We may not have stayed in touch with people from our past but we will still have a large list of people we know. It's worth getting in touch with ex-colleagues, friends from your sports club, etc.

WHO DO YOU KNOW?

You may like to write down the names of everyone you know, so that you can tick their names once you have been in touch with them.

Our wide number of contacts puts us at a huge advantage compared to young people who often say they don't have the connections they need. You will find many people via LinkedIn and Facebook, so search and connect, sending a personalised message on LinkedIn and then following up with something interesting for them.

Let them know that you are seeking advice and ideas. You don't want to ask them if they have a job or they know of a job opening, or the answer is likely to be no and you will have closed the door on the conversation.

I've had clients who tell me they have been networking with a number of people, but they haven't done it effectively.

Case Study

Gary told me how he had met someone for lunch but never really moved the conversation to the job he was looking for or asked for advice. Whilst it was a nice lunch I needed to help him to use this time effectively. This wasn't easy, he said: 'I can understand why you are suggesting that I do this. I need people to help me now; I don't have the time to build connections.' It was much easier for Richard who focused on building connections for more than a year so already had a lot of goodwill he could call on.

Are you networking from behind your computer?

Sitting at your computer is not the same as picking up the phone or getting out and speaking with people in person. People hire people – that's why you need personal connections, chemistry, and fit. It's hard to convey that from behind your computer.

Don't wait till your CV is perfect before you contact people – you can do both in tandem.

The ten-second story

You may have read in other books about the two-minute elevator pitch – what you will say to someone in the two minutes you spend in a lift with them. But really, would you ever launch into a speech? It is very salesy and far too long. Far better to think of a conversation or a story – people like stories, so create an intro that will encourage people to ask questions to find out more. I'd keep it short, just a sentence maybe 10–15 words long.

You need to simply explain what you are looking for and why. This will lead to a discussion and it is through these discussions that we may find out about a job opening or someone may be able to facilitate an introduction. It has to be interesting, and it has to encourage a response from someone else.

If you are out of work and people ask you what you do, avoid answers such as 'I used to be head of sales' . . . or 'I'm an unemployed retail manager.' Use what you have found out about what makes you different; here are some examples.

- *'There are plenty of drivers around, but few take care of parcels and packages like me, I treat everything I deliver as if it is a special gift for the person I'm taking it to.'*
- *'I help customers make choices for clothes and accessories that truly flatter.'*
- *'As an engineer I love to solve problems and use creative techniques to simplify processes.'*

All of these are likely to get a positive response from the person you are talking with. It sounds interesting so they want to know more. You can then follow up with what you are looking for, something like,

'The company I worked for has gone into receivership so I'm now looking for an organisation that would appreciate someone with these personal qualities, do you know anyone?'

The above answer makes it clear what you want, and the person is going to be able to think about how they can help you. Far more powerful than saying 'I don't mind what I do, I just want a job' – this makes it hard for people to help. Christina is clear on what she is looking for:

'My name is Christina Woodcock and I'm an experienced sales manager. I thoroughly enjoy managing people, building relationships and problem-solving. I'm seeking a business sales management role based in Leeds.'

ACTIVITY 25

WRITE DOWN YOUR TEN-SECOND STORY

Take some time to create a first draft.

Building your tribe (connections)

Your 'tribe' are your friends and associates. I discussed this term with my editor, but we agreed that it's used regularly by a younger generation (hipsters) and we need to be familiar with these types of words. To build your tribe (increase your number of contacts) you can try the following six ideas.

1. **Review options in your community.** What do you do outside of work? Do you meet with others through a hobby, religious affiliation, a sport or the gym? Think about where you meet people naturally and if there are ways to expand a conversation to talk about what you are interested in and how they might help you. I go to dance classes and talking with other dancers I learn more about their job and personal situation, so if I can make helpful suggestions I will.
2. **Meet people through your professional association.** There are likely to be regular meetings or occasional conferences, so go to meetings and take on a more active role. Being on the committee or offering to do 'meet and greet' will help in getting to know people. Helping others is a good way to have other people to help us. If you go to a networking event, have a goal or purpose in mind such as to set up two coffee appointments or phone calls from the meeting.

3. **Answer questions on LinkedIn Groups.** A good opportunity to network online – start by reading the posts others make, follow discussions and add value and answer questions to get your name out there. Comment on posts, then ask to connect using a personalised message. Chapter 9, LinkedIn and social media, will help.

4. **Contact recruiters.** Don't just send your CV and ask if you are suitable for any vacancies but tell them that you know they specialise in, for example, engineering recruitment. Tell them you have an extensive network of people who work in this area and if they have vacancies to let you know and you will pass the details on.

5. **Build connections by volunteering.** If you are a web designer, create a website for a voluntary organisation; a graphic designer could create a leaflet for the school fete. Other people will see what you have done and so your expertise is highlighted.

6. **Contact people you know from a long time ago.** If you haven't been in touch with someone (for example, school friends) for many years, then you could get in touch and tell them you were looking at some photos and thought of them and wondered how they were getting on. Most would be delighted to hear from you again.

Network across the generations – seek to build connections with younger people. They may hear of opportunities that people of our generation don't.

When connecting can be helpful

In this section, we will look at four specific times when building personal links can be especially useful.

1. For fact-finding interviews – when you want to find out more about an industry or organisation

There are important reasons to use this type of interview:

- when you have already done a lot of research and now need to talk to someone who has practical experience of a particular job so you can see how well it measures up to your expectations
- when you know what you want to do and are looking for a way to enhance your likelihood of success in getting a job

- when you really want a job in a particular company or industry, and are gathering further intelligence to enhance an application or to make a direct approach.

Most people like to help, so make a personal request and you have a good chance that they will say yes.

Find people to talk with through your connections, including those you have made through LinkedIn. People like to help other people, and a clear request for a short meeting (20 minutes) should lead to at least half of the people you approach saying yes.

You need to be clear why you are getting in touch – you are not asking for a job but seeking to find out more. And you must follow up – you can't expect them to get back to you. It's your priority, not theirs.

Send a short email (or go retro and send a letter!), and follow up with a phone call.

Keep unsolicited emails to less than 200 words. Make them short and to the point and you are more likely to get a response. If they are too long-winded and visually dense, they are less likely to be responded to. Make the email subject line compelling to the target reader.

In your note, be clear about what you want and make it personal so the recipient will want to meet you. Demonstrate that you have already done some research; it's extremely irritating to be asked questions which could have been answered via the internet. If you make your approach personal, so it does not look like something you are sending out to lots of people, you are more likely to get people to say yes. If your approach isn't working, you need to check that you aren't being too pushy. Think from the other person's perspective and write something memorable that will grab their attention.

Here's a real letter from a client that got a meeting.

Dear Geoff,

I have recently spoken with Eric Jackson (who sends his regards), and he recommended I get in touch.

My expertise is supply chain management. I am now considering a move into project management consultancy. My research has identified Jones & Jones as leaders in this field.

My career to date has covered most aspects of customer service and supply chain management. In the recent past I was project manager for a warehouse centralisation project within Schmidt GmbH.

I appreciate you are busy, but would you be able to meet up in person or by Skype for around 20 minutes? Alternatively, I'd be happy to send a couple of questions for you to respond to by email.

I will phone your office next Wednesday.

Best wishes,

David Pearson

Case Study

Katy said: 'I've been following your suggestions to network. I set up a meeting with a lady I had met while freelancing for *Newsweek* and who is an independent consultant working in the publishing industry. She has promised to introduce me to a few of her contacts in the industry. She also suggested a couple of other avenues I might look into. I have also got in touch with a communications manager for a non-profit and will probably meet her next week. I have reworked my CV according to your suggestions. I have also identified a couple of short professional courses I would like to apply to.'

Fact-finding interviews help you build a relationship with someone who works for the organisation you want to work for, and this can help later when you apply for a job or take the direct approach.

Depending on what you find, you could ask to shadow somebody for a day to learn more about a job.

You must undertake comprehensive research in advance, so your questions will focus on what you can't find online rather than waste an opportunity with basic-level questions.

Develop a list of questions; probably six to eight is the maximum you will get covered. Your first fact-finding interview will be broad and general but you will get more specific as you find out more. Have these questions ready before you make your follow-up phone call in case the person wants to go through them over the phone, there and then. You should identify relevant questions to ask through research, but the following examples may also be helpful.

■ What do you do during a typical working day or week?
■ What kind of challenges or problems do you have to deal with in this job?
■ What do you find most satisfying and most frustrating about your job and field?
■ What do you see as the future for this kind of work?
■ In your opinion, what personal qualities are important to being successful in this job?
■ How do you see jobs in this field changing in the future?
■ In your opinion, what are the trends that you see affecting this industry in the future?
■ What do you see as our industry's biggest challenge for the future?

2. To be on an organisation's referral radar
Rather than try to push your way into organisations through job boards and applicant tracking systems (ATS), get pulled into organisations by ex-colleagues who know the quality of your work and how well you will fit in. Find more people, talk to them about the work you do, ask them to pass on your CV or bio and to let you know of opportunities.

A 2014 survey by Jobvite, a recruiting-software provider, found that 63% of jobs are filled via a referral, a huge increase on the 2011 survey data of 29%. The reason for this rise is that there are too many poor-quality applicants who apply online.

Many companies have internal referral programmes in place. They ask their staff to encourage friends and contacts to apply for a job within their company and thereby eliminate the need for the company to conduct a formal search.

There are companies that will even incentivise their staff through money and gifts, with the chance of winning a prize such as a TV or holiday for a successful referral, or an iPad or £1,000 cash bonus for a successful hire.

Multinational corporation Sodexo, a food service and facilities management company that recruits 4,600 managers and executives a year, says that referred employees are ten times more likely to be hired than other applicants.

Companies prefer people who are referred: they are more likely to be better matches, have a mentor within the organisation, are likely to be more productive and to stay longer. People aren't going to suggest someone who won't be successful – it would reflect badly on them – so employers are very satisfied with this approach; 78% of recruiters find their best quality candidates through referrals. This is up from 60% in 2014 (Jobvite survey, 2015).

Obviously a danger is that people refer people like them, sharing the same gender and race and this can include the same age span. At 50+ we should know more people, but we must make sure that we connect with people of different ages, not just the same age as us, and particularly any who work with the company you wish to work for.

Researchers from the Federal Reserve Bank of New York and MIT studied data from a financial services company and found that while referrals only made up about 6% of total applications, they resulted in more than a quarter of those recruited. This was more than the number hired via online job boards, even though those job-hunters accounted for 60% of applications and 40% of interviews. This is likely to be the same in the UK.

As I typed this paragraph, I got a tweet from someone asking if I could suggest anyone for an operations role. It's just like when you seek a builder or a cleaner, you ask around people you know.

3. To find potential opportunities or leads

With a list of 50 companies to target, you can focus your attention on these. You can then ask people if they know anyone who works for these organisations.

Ask for advice on possible job openings or how to increase your chance of a successful application. If you don't hear back, contact them again to ask if they have any other ideas. If you wait, the other person will get busy, feel guilty and think that if you were still interested you would have got back in touch.

Consider where the people who work in the place you want to work hang out. Then make sure to hang out where they hang out!

4. Just before applying

Using LinkedIn provides an excellent way of making contact with people to help you research your application. Once you have found someone, you can send a message such as the following.

> *Hi, my name is (name) and I'm researching the XYZ Company. I know you used to work there because (explain). I'm considering making an application. Would you be able to answer a couple of questions to help me to see if it would be worthwhile? I know this is an unusual approach but I want my application to stand out.*

If they say no, ask if they can suggest anyone you should be talking with.

Chances are you will get some great material, and you can follow up with someone else to find out more. From this you can see how well you meet the needs of an employer, some of their challenges, the inside scoop on how the industry is going, etc. This may include not pursuing an application, but better to find this information out now than invest too much time and energy in an application.

You can use this information to enhance your application and to check out your assumptions about the job and requirements of the organisation. Find out more about the customer perspective and Problems, Issues, Needs and Trends (PINTs!). Ask questions that you actually want to find out about and that relate to what you can contribute to the organisation.

Through your contacts you should be able to find people who used to work at this company in the past. Be sociable and ask these people how they liked working there. Notice if there is any hesitation before they answer. The pause may be a clue that they don't want to answer negatively and are framing a safe answer.

Possible questions you could ask may include the following.

About the manager
- Did you work directly for (name of potential boss)?
- What is (name) like? – What they mention first will be a key characteristic. You may need to ask follow-up questions.
- What does this manager look for in an employee? – Then ask them to consider how their experience compares to that of the people normally recruited.

About the department
- What are the department's biggest issues?
- Is the department respected by the rest of the company?
- Is the department seen as adding value to the company or is it viewed as just another cost centre?
- What's the biggest thing the department needs to do to be successful?

About the company
- If there's one thing they need to do better than their competitors, what is it?
- What do they do better than their competitors?
- Who are their best customers?
- Can you think of anyone else I should talk to?
- Why did you leave?

When you find an advertised job you can also use your connections. Ask them to personally hand over your CV/application to the person who would be your line manager and you may get fast-tracked through the ATS shortlisting process.

Practical guidance

Phone call
Remember when we used to pick up the phone and talk? Now connections are most likely to be via email or Messenger. We often like these as we can

be well prepared over what we want to say. But phoning someone can lead to an instant response and is the best way of arranging a time to meet – you can both have your diaries handy.

Making these calls can be a bit stressful, especially the first time, so breathe deeply and act positive and upbeat. If you stand up when you speak, it keeps your energy up and you will come across as more confident.

If you are going to phone, you may find it helpful to have a script as a reminder. You mustn't read it line by line – it mustn't sound like a script, so you may need to practise several times so that it sounds natural. Here's a suggestion – we anticipated a couple of responses.

Start with an introduction.

'I'm doing research into (name the organisation's business, e.g. charity marketing) and my research suggested your organisation has a strong reputation (or is a market leader). Could you spare 20 minutes at the end of the day to answer some questions?'

'What specifically would you like to find out?'

'The challenges facing the sector and the types of charity that are likely to appreciate someone with my background in the comms industry. An introduction to some charities would be brilliant. I've identified about six charities I'd like to approach, plus I have a list of questions.'

'Why not email me your list so I can see who I know there and I'll answer your questions by email.'

'Thank you, I'll get the list emailed over later today and could we then meet up in a couple of weeks?'

'Yes, that's fine.'

You may feel a little shy about making the call, but most people want to help.

If you arrange to meet, suggest a coffee (with you picking up the bill). Somewhere close to their place of work is likely to work best, and if you have requested 20 minutes, make sure you stick to the time limit.

At the meeting

The aim of a fact-finding interview is to find out more about a potential career, or to learn more to increase your chance of success.

The interview will also allow you to:

- show them that you value their time by being prepared; have your questions ready
- ask for feedback on your CV, qualifications and proposed direction
- ask for contacts who could help with advice and suggestions (NOT to request jobs from) and ideally for them to introduce you to them
- ask permission to use the interviewer's name as an introduction if you are to contact them yourself
- ask if you can help them in any way
- ask permission to keep the interviewer informed of the progress you make.

Make sure they know you are seeking advice, so ask questions and make notes. Listen carefully to what they say, they may tell you about new changes within the industry, e.g. that a company may be expanding.

When you meet with people make sure to ask questions of them – if they start asking you questions, provide some detail but then flip the question and ask them about themselves and their work. If a meeting leads to a referral this is a very positive result, and make sure to follow up with a thank-you note. At other times it won't lead to anything, but don't think it never will: keep in touch every six weeks or so.

Go into the meeting focused on finding out as much as you can about the other person and their organisation. Don't try to sell yourself but ask intelligent questions and answer their questions and show you would be a great colleague.

Throughout the meeting you want to use effective body language and non-verbal behaviour; talking with a similar voice tone and having a similar posture can help to build rapport. Being friendly and smiling will be helpful.

Towards the end of the meeting after you've thanked the individual for their time and effort, you might say:

'I've learnt a great deal today. Having heard about your organisation, I'm interested in talking to more people about this field. I'm especially interested in (any special area that came up during your meeting). Who do you think I should talk with next?'

Be sure to phrase it that way. This is positive and assumes that they know someone as opposed to 'Can you think of anyone I should talk with next?'

Afterwards send a thank-you note. Also, review how the meeting went. Review both the information you gained, and also how you came across. How can you improve for next time?

IN A NUTSHELL

You should be much clearer on the need to connect with people you know and the need to grow your connections, especially with people outside your usual circle. You know the job you seek and the companies where you would like to work. Build these connections so you may get referred for a job opening.

You've learnt, too, that you need to meet with people, not to focus on online networking alone. Now plan how you will use your connections – for fact-finding interviews, to learn more about organisations to enhance your application, and especially to be on their radar.

Connections are going to enhance your direct approach so fast-forward to Chapter 11 if you are ready for this now.

BEFORE YOU MOVE ON

- Make a note of three key points you have learnt.
- Make a note of what is the top takeaway, for you, from this chapter.

- **Who are you now going to contact? Create a plan and get in touch.**

8 21ST-CENTURY CVs

Too many people make fatal mistakes with their CV, such as not amending their CV for different applications. Make sure your CV is targeted for the job you want, choose the right examples and use the right key words.

In this chapter you will address these points and:

■ take a critical view of your CV and make sure that it is ready for a 21st-century job search and not stuck in a time warp

■ learn about the importance of key words, and how you need to create a CV that will get through ATS software as well as a human sift.

You have worked through earlier chapters and are now clear on the type of job you are looking for. This gives focus for your CV. Without this focus your CV will be bland, and is unlikely to meet the needs of any of the jobs you apply for. If you have more than one career objective, then you will need two or more CVs.

The nine-second review

Career professionals used to write that a recruiter would give a CV a one- or two-minute skim-read before a decision was made. Partly down to social media like Twitter, this time has now dropped to about nine seconds. This means that you need to immediately grab the reader's attention, particularly when they look at the top half of your CV. This is what will appear on a computer screen before the reader scrolls down. I spoke with a recruiter recently to ask how she manages to read a CV so quickly. She told me that she doesn't actually read them, but scans them and she is looking for reasons to reject a candidate as much as to add them to the read pile.

Reasons your CV can be discarded by recruiters

- **Typos and length** – Obvious typos, grammatical errors and long and hard-to-read CVs mean a high chance of rejection.
- **Industry** – Their client wants a perfect match, ideally someone who is already doing the same job for a competitor, so if you don't clearly match up, for example you have worked in finance in the public sector but they want to fill a vacancy in the private sector, or you have worked in distribution and they want experience from a retail background, your chance of success is slim.
- **Location** – If the job is based in London and you live outside a commutable area you will be out. Most companies have no intention of relocating someone for a job. If you want to move location, be smart and omit location against your current job and take your postcode off your CV.
- **Level** – If the advertised job is for a senior manager and your job title does not include 'senior' you are unlikely to be shortlisted. You may also be rejected if your career history shows you as too senior for the specific vacancy.
- **Recent experience** – You may have worked in sales training but if it was more than five years ago, it doesn't count for much. Recruiters want you to have recent experience. This doesn't help Sue who was considering a return to something she'd done 15 years ago before becoming self-employed. She needs to contact companies direct, not expect to get shortlisted.

- **Education** – If the employer wants someone with a degree and you don't have one, this is another reason to get your application discarded. It can also work the other way and a PhD shows you as overqualified for the job. You can address this by including 'degree calibre' on your CV. Back in the 1970s very few people went to university, born 30 years later and you probably would have a degree, so address it like this.
- **How many jobs?** – You may have had to take on short-term contracts, so make this clear on your CV or it looks like you can't hold down a job. No-one wants a job-hopper.
- **Combination CV** – Recruiters don't like these CVs – they think you are trying to hide something. This type of CV works much better when not used for mass recruitment, so you may need to have two styles of CV.

The aim of your CV is to get to someone who can make a decision to invite you to interview. It does not need to be a detailed description of everything you have done in a 30-year work history.

When emailed, your CV may be reviewed on a phone, so it has to be readable on a 5.5-inch screen. And please make sure it can be opened without having to, for example, go into Google Docs – that will just increase the chance of your CV being deleted.

Let's review your CV

Is your CV stuck in a time warp?
Far too many people are using CVs that belong in a museum; they are using the same style from 20 years ago. This doesn't just affect those of us who are 50+; I've worked with a client of 36 who was in her last job for 11 years so her CV was from when she was 25. Styles change, so get yours up to date.

Grab your CV and let's take a critical stance. Imagine you are shortlisting for the job you seek; would you shortlist you? We will review your CV section by section, but let's first take an overall view.

Given that only limited attention will be paid to your CV, you shouldn't try to include everything you can. Focus your details on what is relevant to **this particular job**. The general view is that two sides of A4 is correct; occasionally a very senior executive may have three sides but only provide a longer CV when it is absolutely essential.

Poor Gary, he sent me his four-page CV which was headed Curriculum Vitae. There were ten separate lines at the top covering a lot of personal detail and long lists of detail under each job. His education included being at secondary school from 1970 to 1976 and even his primary school details. Far too much was irrelevant and it was clear why he wasn't getting shortlisted.

Ensure your CV makes it clear why you are a great fit for the job. When compared to other people applying for a similar job, does yours stand out because you are clear on how you add value? Your work in Chapter 4 will be helpful here.

Professional Advice

Regardless of your age, employers are looking for people who will fit in well and do the job that needs to be done. Personalising your letter and CV to their needs, circumstances and values will go a long way to getting you an interview – rather than sending your standard CV and speculative letter. Personalising also allows you to showcase your wealth of experience – and helps employers see your individuality.

Show potential employers that you've taken the time to really consider your application because you want to work for them and the reasons why your experiences fit in with what they are looking for and make you the stand-out candidate. And then if you get an interview, continue that approach by spending time researching the company before the interview. Websites contain a lot of information about the culture, values and the way they run themselves that will help you understand what they are looking for, and help you stand out from the crowd.

Jacquie Wiggett, director of HR and
organisational development at the Financial Ombudsman Service

---

To bring your CV up to date you should include

■ **A headline statement.** Include your top strengths at the top of your CV either directly under your name or in a short opening statement. You don't need to spell out the detail that will be included in the rest of your CV. If you are a financial planner start with that, don't lose it in a long statement. I like to include something like 'Project Management Expert' directly under a person's name on their CV. Or choose your top three or four key words with a divider such as 'I' in between, to define your main focus. See Anita's example on page 97.

- **Professional highlights.** This highlights your best assets for the job you are seeking. Make it short and snappy bullets not a dense paragraph.
- **Some colour.** Either in a border or to pull out your name and headings, but don't overdo it.
- **Metrics and examples to back up what you say**. You think you are a great team player, but you must give evidence. You could also **include a graph or two** to highlight key numerical data.
- **Start with what's key.** Each bullet should start with what's most important, and can also be highlighted in bold, just like a newspaper headline.
- **Key words.** Related to your industry and the particular job you seek.
- **A modern font and a clear layout**. Times New Roman looks old-fashioned. Use a modern sans-serif font like Arial, Calibri or Tahoma. Don't put narrow margins – you need to have some white space.
- **Focus on the past 10–15 years.** You don't need to go back to the 1970s – that dates you. If you need to include details from your earlier career, include this in an 'Earlier Career' section or use this information in a combination CV with details on the first page which presents examples against key headings.
- **Make your job title bold, not the employer:**

Head of Procurement, ACME Consulting   Oct 2010 – Mar 2016

Streamlined end-to-end process for invoicing and billing onto clients by working with vendors on electronic invoice for major suppliers.

And avoid

- **An objective.** CVs have changed and you no longer need the objective statement at the top, focused on what you want (i.e. 'seeking a challenging position as Head of Procurement where I can use my skills …'). Instead your CV is a marketing document, focused on the needs of the person who initially will shortlist you and later interview you. The hiring manager doesn't care what you want, only if you are going to help him or her solve problems, make money, whatever is required in the job.

- **Long descriptions of tasks and duties.** You need to focus more on telling your career story. This is not where you copy in your job description. It's less about a list of tasks and more about what that task resulted in, what you achieved. As you write about your employment history are you making clear what you have delivered through your achievement bullets? The focus is on your accomplishments and the contribution you have made to the organisation's bottom line.

- **'References are available upon request.'** It's expected you will supply these when asked.

- **Hobbies.** Don't include, unless related to the job or something that will really pique their interest.

- **Personal information.** Marital status, number of children, NI number, all can be omitted.

- **Leaving gaps on your CV.** Include details of voluntary work or care activity.

Case Study

Suzanne used this advice to make some changes to her CV, such as to exclude full details of jobs prior to 2004, the dates of her earlier (less relevant) degrees, coaching qualifications, interests and references being available. She said: 'Having been used to a more traditional form of CV, some of this has taken a bit of getting used to!'

Use key words

You must use enough of the right key words. Pay close attention to the job ad but don't just copy what's included. CVs that match too closely are treated with suspicion. It's better to paraphrase and use similar words. If you aren't sure what words to include, start by reviewing the job profiles on the National Careers Service website, also look at job adverts and job sites showing job profiles.

You can also identify relevant words through looking at the company's website. Organisations use words differently so look for the ways they describe key qualities and values. Using similar language will help show you as a good fit.

Don't just stuff your CV full of 'buzz words' like hard-worker and self-starter but include words relevant for the job you are targeting. You may need to be a bit creative, so for example if you don't have membership of the Chartered Institute of Marketing (CIM) you could include 'working towards membership of the Chartered Institute of Marketing (CIM)'.

Remember, if you get shortlisted you will need to be able to provide an example to back up each key word you have included.

Professional development

Young people will focus on their education. That's far less important to us than the evidence that we keep our skills updated.

I prefer this heading to 'Education' and you can adapt it to, for example, 'Professional sales development' if you work in sales and have done excellent courses, such as with Anthony Robbins.

If our formal education ended 20 years ago, we can omit dates from our degree. If you don't have a degree you could say something like 'educated to A level standard' or 'educated to GCSE level'. As we get older, A levels, etc. are less likely to be relevant, but are worth including if gained as a mature student.

What will be more important is to **show how we keep our skills updated and invested in our professional development** so include details of short courses attended. Definitely include those which are relevant to the job you seek, but you can also include other courses that demonstrate your willingness to learn new things.

I encourage clients to look at edX for short courses such as 'Communicating Strategically', which is aimed at scientists, or to search for MOOCs. These are short courses that can help us to develop our knowledge and enhance our CVs. See Chapter 16, Staying employable, for more details.

Employers expect certain technical skills, such as the ability to use Word and Excel, so these are generally not seen as anything special. For most jobs if you don't have strong skills in these areas, you will need to learn.

How are your languages? This could help you to stand out. If you have a reasonable level of fluency it is worth mentioning it, but don't fib or you may find yourself being asked questions in the language you claim fluency in.

Professional memberships

If you have gained membership of organisations such as the Institute of Marketing, or are a chartered engineer, include details. You don't need to say when the membership was gained.

Interests

It's debatable whether you should include these. You may share an interest with the person reviewing your CV or they may take a negative view on what is listed. As someone over 50, we may like to refer to activities like dancing, running or swimming that indicate our fitness levels, or learning a language to show we are able to learn new things. However, rather than write 'running', expand it to, for example, 'training to complete a half marathon in the spring'.

Once you have all the text, you can then look at style. Add a border, some graphs and call-out boxes of text, but if your CV is being uploaded and will go through ATS software be aware that this information may not be seen as the software can't cope with boxes and images, so two versions of your CV are useful.

Different styles of CV

When you are looking for a job that is of a similar type to those you have already done, then a chronological CV will be perfect. If you are seeking a career change, however, or have had substantial time away from the work place, you can take a different approach and use a combination CV.

The chronological CV

Choose this if you have a steady record of employment in an industry or functional area and want to stay in the same line of work.

The combination (skills-based) CV

With this type of CV most of the first page lists relevant examples under the key requirements of the job, thus making it easy for someone to see how you will match up. The second side will include your career history with some brief details under each job. This style addresses the key problem found in true skills-based CVs which hide the actual work history.

The chronological CV

Let's look at this in sections, starting with your contact details.

Contact details

Resist the urge to head it with anything except your name and don't fill a quarter of the page with your contact details on separate lines, as Gary did. The top of your CV can look something like this.

Anita Watson
Legal Executive
Focused on customers and profit

Chester CH3
07931 303 367
www.linkedin.com/in/anitawatson2
anitawatson414@gmail.com

There is no need to include your postal address, partly down to identity fraud when CVs are uploaded, as all correspondence will be by email. Review the email address you use. If you use, for example, ngraham1957@gmail.com that's a good indicator of the year you were born. Too many people send applications from the fun/jokey address they use for communicating with friends, such as fabgranny@yahoo.co.uk or grumpydon@gmail.com. Keep these for your personal contacts, and for work use a more professional email address such as dk.taylor248@gmail.com. It has been reported that more than 75% of CVs are ignored if the email address is unprofessional. If you still use a @AOL account you may like to get a Gmail account for your job search, as AOL can appear old-fashioned and suggests you are 50+.

You don't need to label your phone number and email – it's obvious. Your mobile number means you are accessible, but you must have a professional voicemail message. A younger client would rarely quote a landline number, so you can omit this. In most cases also include your LinkedIn URL. Make sure you have a personalised (and professional) voicemail message; you want anyone who calls you to be clear they have got through to the right person.

You can include your job title under your name it makes the type of work you are targeting clear. One's eye is drawn to this alongside your name, thus giving a favourable impression. Expand it, too, with an additional description like Anita has done above.

Name and contact details are clearly laid out and the link to the LinkedIn profile is available so the reader can quickly find out more about you. There is no need to include your national insurance number, marital status, driving licence details, etc., here like Gary did; you would be wasting the most important space on your CV.

Grab their attention

This next section of the CV is where most people put their career objective, focused on what they want and including a lot of bland generic terms. Change the focus to how you can add value to the organisation – it's a taster for what you will include in your cover letter, to make them want to meet you. Make it succinct and pertinent to the job. Focus on strengths, your value proposition and top skills that relate to the job in question. The way you meet their requirements should be easy to spot.

You may have 25 years' experience as a management accountant but list it as 15+ years to avoid shouting out your age.

Phil used the following introduction:

> *Highly accomplished operations manager with a 10+ years' successful track record of consistently increasing revenue and slashing operating costs. Track record of excellent customer focus and increasing profitability in all areas of the business – money, staff morale, and environmental impact.*

Think of this section as a standalone bio – would it make you want to read further?

> **Case Study**
> Ideally, Pat would become a 'serious games' designer and said that his USP is that he is a good teacher combined with years of software-development experience, and interdisciplinary interests.

You will have identified the key skills for the job you seek. Use this section to make it clear that you have these skills. You can list these skills in three or four columns.

Mergers and Acquisitions	Revenue generation New product	Regulatory Compliance
Visionary leadership	development	Debt/equity financing

But don't just list key words in a skills section, these key words need to be included throughout your CV.

Experience section
Whilst most people will head this section 'Career' or 'Work History', you could use this heading to emphasise your expertise. You could focus it on the job you seek or your career history overview, for example 'Sales achievements and performance', 'Technical leadership experience' or 'Operations management career'. Start with your current or most recent job and include the dates on a separate line (these can be full years). Then provide details on previous jobs.

If the company is not well known include a _brief_ description of the company, the area in which it trades, size and revenue details. Take two lines maximum. For example:

XXXXXXXX is a Clinical Research Organisation which conducts clinical trials

You can change the job title! Job titles can be misleading. If yours is particular to your organisation, provide the more generic title.

Think about what is right for the job you seek. Remember, you don't need to include everything back to your first job in the 1970s – don't go back more than 10–15 years. You can summarise first jobs in an 'Earlier Career' segment, and if some of these jobs are more relevant, you may be better off using the combination-style CV.

It's tempting to write that you have 25 years' experience in a particular area, but you will never see a job description that asks for more than ten years' experience (possibly 15 for senior positions), so better to note it as 10+ years.

If you have spent 18 years working for one company, show your career progression by including different jobs as separate entries. If you have had to take a number of short-term jobs which don't follow on from your earlier career history, group them together so they don't take the focus away from what you want to get back to.

Achievement bullets

Most CVs end up as a job description describing what we have done, rather than how well we have done it, and too many go back too far. I still see CVs that list detail from the job description, and when I ask why they haven't included achievement bullets, Gary and others say they are difficult to write. But you have to invest the time in this, that's what is expected. What can help is to review each job and to think about CAR – the **challenges** you had, the **action** you took and the **results** that happened. Think about how you made a difference.

We create value in our job in different ways. We may not win a half-million-pound contract but we can be brilliant health and safety inspectors and save our company millions through ensuring people are safe and accidents do not occur. We could go that extra mile by providing a high level of customer care on the service desk at the garage, so customers come back each time their car needs a service and buy their next car from our company too. Think of examples similar to these to enhance this section of your CV.

Write down details of each job you have had, including short-term assignments. As preparation, it helps to list all your jobs from leaving education; not that you will include them on your CV but so you can refer to this list if you ever need precise dates. It will also identify any gaps that you may need to explain.

Now you have your list of jobs, you can start thinking about the tasks you did. To create an effective CV you need to go beyond the list of tasks you did and focus on the impact on the company. I'm forever asking my clients, **'And what did that result in?'**

Think about the different tasks you have done in your last job. Think of a problem you have had to solve or an opportunity you have taken advantage of. Which of your skills or strengths did you use, or what expertise? What was the benefit of this action? Is it possible to quantify what you did – did you save or make money or time, or reduce staffing costs? Start writing these down!

What impact did the work have on the companies? Did you solve a problem, save money, make money, and improve efficiency? You must be able to communicate the impact and return on investment of your performance.

You must address the **so what?** Be clear on the relevance of everything you include on your CV. You managed a team of ten – OK, but how did you manage differently, what did your team achieve that was down to your leadership?

Excellent oral and written communication skills is another – so what! This needs to be revised. Make a memorable story such as 'Wrote and presented successful training seminars to 112 customer-service advisors resulting in an increase in customer satisfaction of 18% over the next three-month period.'

Use the present tense for your current job. Write in the past tense for previous jobs.

You should aim to **include three or four bullets under each job;** perhaps up to six for your most recent job and fewer for earlier ones. Throughout, review what you have included and **look for the link between this job and the job you are applying for**. Also, keep them to a maximum of three lines, and ideally two, otherwise they are paragraphs.

It helps to simplify what you write, so rather than 'increased sales revenue by £450,000 in 2015 by generating and implementing strategies to renew the team's strategic focus on the accounts producing the most sales volume', *phew!*, swap it for 'grew annual sales by £450k by refocusing team on the company's most lucrative accounts'.

The focus is on achievements, not a list of duties and responsibilities. Achievements should also have a numerical element where possible, so you include details of income earned, money saved, etc. It's not possible for every job, but do make sure you are focused on what you actually achieved.

Too often, people fail to emphasise their strengths. For example, writing 'duties included supervision of staff' would have a much stronger impact if written as 'successfully led a team of six, providing leadership and coaching which resulted in us being commended on our work by the MD'. Instead of 'excellent communication skills', change to 'complimented on my presentational skills, which included leading the winning pitch for a £50k project for my company'.

Sometimes it may feel appropriate to include a link to some online information, perhaps an example of your work, but this takes time and you must motivate the reader to want to click and read. Far better to include details within your CV.

Language is important. **Avoid cliché phrases** such as 'a team player who is able to work alone' – you must **provide specific examples.**

Make sure the examples include key words to increase the likelihood of being matched with a particular job. I've described earlier how to identify relevant key words. A couple of examples of achievement bullets should emphasise what's required.

- Worked with staff and associates to increase product turnover by 15% and sales by 23%.
- Trained 14 new employees, five of whom were rapidly promoted. Devised and implemented a new sales training programme which resulted in a 37% increase in new business.

It can be done. I took some very brief bullet points that Suzanne included and asked some questions to help her to develop these bullets further.

- **Taught general English classes at various levels.** – What levels? How many classes? What was some specific challenge or great success that you could include?
- **Assessed new students.** – How many students? How did you assess them? What did this lead to?
- **Led social activities.** – Can you give some more detail about what you did and how this helped?

Case Study

I appreciate this can be difficult for some. For example, Suzanne says: 'I can't say how many students I've "successfully" taught or exactly how many passed their exams. I've focused on the wide range of teaching and other experience I have, particularly from my most recent job. Although language schools exist to make money and want teachers who will keep students coming back and recommending the school to others, it's difficult to measure the extent to which I've done that. I haven't won any awards or noticeably had the best feedback in the school. I just know that generally students are satisfied with my teaching and in some cases they're very happy! I'm not sure how to best reflect that in a CV.'

We were able to add more value to the bullets on her CV. What Suzanne had originally written is in bold and you can see how we extended each bullet.

- **Taught general English classes** at all levels from A1 to B2; group classes and one-to-one tuition.
- **Assessed new students** to allocate them to the right class.
- Acted as a buddy for teachers who were new to the school and gave support and encouragement to inexperienced teachers.
- **Led social activities** outside the school, to places like the National Portrait Gallery, to enable students to practise English in a social setting and learn about British culture, and pizza-making and trips to local cafes, to enable students to practise their English while having fun and socialising.

Short-term assignments

As you list your career history, some of the work may have been as a temp. If you got the assignment via an agency, it is the agency that you worked for, not the company where you were assigned.

You may be like Rachael and have found yourself working on short-term assignments. Nilesh, too, worked for four companies in two years in his role as management accountant, due to taking on short-term contracts. He wanted to downplay this time as other jobs had lasted for three years or more, so on his CV he wrote:

2013–2015 Management Accountant

During this period, key positions were held with several large companies on fixed-term contracts including working with (company name) and (company name).

In some cases it might be better to include temporary work as if you were a consultant or freelance worker. It works well if the temporary work you were doing has little relevance to the job you seek, as you can adjust the description of the work more easily. (Temporary work can often be a step along the way to a permanent job.)

Voluntary work

People are often unsure where to include voluntary work – within their work history or in a separate section. For most people, including it in their employment history will be the best place, but please make sure you indicate that it is voluntary and not salaried.

Previous jobs

List previous jobs in reverse chronological order. If there are gaps, you may prefer to include dates in years and omit months. If you have had a lot of jobs, including the dates on the right-hand side means they don't come across as important, as we read from left to right. Follow the same format as with your current job.

Don't leave a gap. Include details on what you did, such as volunteering or caring.

If you have a career history spanning more than 15 years it's unlikely that your earlier career is relevant, so group earlier details together.

Review this section. It may well be too long, so you will want to edit carefully. Choose the highlights, only include what is most relevant to the job and the examples that are most likely to get you shortlisted.

Information can be presented in a very boring way, so spend some time thinking of ways you can enhance what you say. Instead of saying 'managed day-to-day network operations' you could say: 'averted numerous cyber-attacks by employing state-of-the-art cyber security'. You can include numerical data in a graph to add visual impact to your CV.

For everything on the CV we should ask 'So what?', What does that mean?, Will it help me to be shortlisted for the job?

Make sure you describe things using current terminology – avoid calling yourself a typist or secretary, for example; call yourself an admin assistant.

The combination (skills-based) CV

This style of CV will allow you to focus on how well you match up to the requirements of the job. It's useful to take the emphasis off a recent career history of low-paid jobs, or when you want to move into a new area, and to include examples from your non-work life. This is the style I suggest to many, especially when people want a change of occupation. It worked very well for Nilesh, and also for Sue and Rachael.

Let me talk you through how Nilesh used this approach. We've identified school business manager as a good move for him. He first noted the skills and knowledge required for this role, found on the National Careers Service website:

- experience in management, accounting or finance
- excellent speaking and writing skills
- the ability to lead teams of staff in different departments
- planning and decision-making skills
- the ability to manage large budgets
- good organisation and time management
- the ability to stay calm under pressure and meet strict deadlines
- computer skills including use of spreadsheet programs

Instead of a conventional layout, Nilesh uses the points above as the basis for the headings on page 1 of his CV. Under each, he gives examples of how his background meets that requirement.

This type of CV needs to be adapted to the needs of a particular application so when he applies for a job as bursar with a sixth-form college the job ad states the following requirements for skills and expertise:

- budget management
- communication skills
- Microsoft Office
- project management
- staff management

Page 2 lists his career history, which he keeps brief. Alongside job title, employer, and dates, there is a short summary of each job. He still includes details of his education and training, as in a chronological CV, and again omits the dates.

Nilesh Shah
School Business Manager

address
name@gmail.com
LinkedIn

Opening Statement: You can either write one or two short paragraphs summarising in general terms key highlights or you can show as a list of key words laid out over three or four columns, just don't use both styles.

| Key word 1 | Key word 3 | Key word 5 | Key word 7 |
| Key word 2 | Key word 4 | Key word 6 | Key word 8 |

Achievement Highlights

Team Management
- Example 1 – each example can take one to two lines (if it goes onto three lines it will be a paragraph, not a bullet).
- Example 2 – these are specific examples drawn from your career history and out of work life; you don't need to say where the example is from.
- Example 3 – three examples seems about right, but two to four is fine; it all depends on how much can fit onto a two-sided CV.

Accounting and Finance
- Example 1
- Example 2
- Example 3

Planning and Decision-making
- Example 1
- Example 2
- Example 3

Budget Management
- Example 1
- Example 2
- Example 3

Computer Skills
- If this is included in the job and you want to confirm your competence with, for example, Microsoft Office.
- Keep it brief, this is unlikely to be the key competence to share.

Personal Qualities
- Based on this particular application and job requirements, this section will need to include details on organisational skills and time management, and the ability to stay calm under pressure and meet deadlines. There could be one bullet related to each of these.
- Depending on the personal qualities, this might be split into two, or you may realise that not everything can be addressed here and instead include details in the key words section above.

nshah_p1

Career History/Professional Expertise

Job Title, Organisation   Dates
- It is the job title that is bold, not the organisation. You may decide to put dates on the line below but aligned to the right.
- Under this and other jobs you include one or two bullets with specific achievements for this particular job.

Job Title, Organisation   Dates
- XXXXXXXXXXXXXXXXXXXXXXXXXXXXXXXXXXXXXXX.
- XXXXXXXXXXXXXXXXXXXXXXXXXXXXXXXXXXXXXXXXXXXXXXXXXXXXXXXXXXXXXXXXXXXXXXX XXXXXXXXXXXXXXXXXXXXXXXXXXXXXXXXXXXXXXXXXXX

Job Title, Organisation   Dates
- XXXXXXXXXXXXXXXXXXXXXXXXXXXXXXXXXXXXXXX.
- XXXXXXXXXXXXXXXXXXXXXXXXXXXXXXXXXXXXXXXXXXXXXXXXXXXXXXXXXXXXXXXXXXXXXXX XXXXXXXXXXXXXXXXXXXXXXXXXXXXXXXXXXXXXXXXXXX

Previous Employment History
- No need to include dates here.
- You can group together previous employment into one section.
- You don't need to go back to when you were 16 – you can say something like 'a number of admin and junior management positions'.

Education and Development
- No need to include dates here.
- Degree – and if you don't have a degree you can say 'degree calibre'.
- Certificate – it's not just degrees, add other relevant courses.
- Short course – it's helpful to include a few of your most recent courses to show that you like to keep your knowledge up to date. Include dates.

nshah_p2

Applying online/Applicant Tracking System (ATS) software

A CV used to be sent by mail, later by email in response to a job ad. Mainly we now apply online and need a CV that is uploadable. In most cases your CV will need to get through an initial, automated sift; the decision will be made by technology, not a real person. Most large employers use applicant tracking system (ATS) software to sift out who to shortlist. To get through this sift you need specific key words in your CV that show a good fit with the job description. But you can't just stuff your CV with key words, they have to make sense in how they are presented for when your CV is reviewed by a real person.

You will be able to write in more detail in your LinkedIn profile, but with your CV every word counts. You must make sure the key information is clear and stands out – use shorter bullets that tell your career story concisely. Much of the information in your CV will also be included in your LinkedIn profile, so you will want to ensure that the content matches, not using the same words but making sure that the detail underlying each, especially dates, is the same.

Organisations use ATS software to manage the high volume of applicants who apply for jobs that are advertised online. Many applicants are poorly qualified for jobs they apply for and there just isn't the time to skim-read all applications. The ATS software scans for key words related to a particular job.

That's why key words are so important. Of course the software may miss well qualified candidates who don't include enough key words, but as long as they find a qualified candidate they are happy. Another reason for using this system is that the organisation can prove that it is not discriminating against people, as it is the ATS system which has shortlisted candidates.

This is still a recent change and most of my clients, of all ages, are unaware of how ATS software works so here's an overview of the five stages.

1. Your CV is uploaded or sent to HR.
2. A computer program removes formatting.
3. Key words are used to search for candidates who match.
4. Your CV is scored based on relevancy.
5. Your CV will then be reviewed by a human.

ATS systems don't like skills-based CVs as they are set up to digest chronological formats. So you may need a conventional CV for when the software will review your application.

Make sure you also include related words and focus on priority words found in the company's listed job title and in the description headlines. Especially use any words found more than twice. Also include key words related to your experience, qualifications and perhaps even the name of a competitor.

> **Case Study**
>
> Richard was very pleased with the skills-based CV we created but found he wasn't getting shortlisted when he applied online. When he produced a highly targeted biographical CV he began to get shortlisted, although he found taking direct action much more effective.

Key words should be included throughout your CV and need to be specific, so list specific terms. If the job ad says ten years' experience, you need to include your 15 years of experience as 10+ years, as the software is looking for this specific number.

> **Case Study**
>
> Suzanne said: 'I haven't yet made any changes in relation to ATS software. This is partly because of time but also because I don't know if the schools I'll be applying to are likely to use it.' Suzanne is right, this isn't likely to be relevant to her, but choosing key words should still be.

Finding the right key words
Follow these steps for a quick and easy key-word-research technique.

Step 1: Find out what words employers use
Key words can be verbs, nouns and job-specific terms: soft skills such as dealing with people, communication, creativity, problem-solving, and leadership. Hard skills are technical or procedural. You can find these by looking at job titles, products or services, job responsibilities, qualifications and software. You can also identify relevant words through looking at the company's website. Organisations use words differently so look for the ways they describe key qualities and values. Using similar language will help show you as a good fit.

Take the job title of the job you seek, visit a job site and see how employers are talking about that job. For example, if you want to get a job as a technical programme manager enter that title into a job site (e.g. Monster) and click on the first two or three results, pasting them into a blank document. Then do the same for several other job boards, like Indeed and Simply Hired. By the end of this step, you will have a document with six to nine technical programme manager job descriptions.

Step 2: Grab the commonly used words visually

Copy all the text into a word-cloud generator e.g. tagcrowd.com, worditout.com or wordle.net and the top words will appear. If some of the skills are two words but are commonly hyphenated, such as problem-solving, make sure to include the hyphen or they will be treated as separate words.

You can clearly see the words 'procurement', 'supplier', 'facilities' and 'plan', so you would want to make sure that these words are included throughout your CV.

Make sure it reads naturally; you can't just include key words that make little sense to a reader.

There may be different ways to describe your job, or aspects of your job; think of as many as possible, as any or all may be relevant. You can also look at ads for similar jobs to see what's included.

Step 3: Review headings

The ATS software expects to see headings such as Experience, Professional Experience, and Education, so if you usually use creative headings, for this you need to use more conventional ones.

Step 4: Create a summary section

The ATS is looking for a summary section (not a boring profile of what *you* want), so write one which includes the value you bring and also details on how you will increase profits, decrease expenses, exceed targets, etc.

Create a .txt file

To make your CV as easy as possible for the ATS software to read, create a .txt file. This omits any advanced formatting such as boxes, borders, tables and images. Starting with a plain text version means you won't get unusual symbols as the job-site software strips out your formatting.

To create a text-based CV, don't play about with your Word document; instead save your CV as a plain text file or copy it into a text-editing program such as Notepad. Once you open it, all formatting such as underlines, bold, fonts, etc. will have been stripped away.

You can then improve the layout by using a hard return (use the 'Enter' key to start a new line). Otherwise, whilst it might look OK in a word-processing program, it can be very difficult to read via a text package without hard returns. You can make improvements to the style if you use CAPITAL LETTERS as headers.

The final review

Now you have completed your CV, leave it for at least 24 hours and then come back and review it. Ask yourself the following questions.

- **Is it focused on the job I'm applying for?**
  Do you need to tweak your examples? You must target your CV to make sure that the reader feels that you have written directly to them, you understand their problems and you are able to solve them.
- **Is it concise and clear?**
  Make sure every word helps make the pitch. If your CV covers a page and a half, do not be tempted to fill the space.
- **Does it grab attention?**
  Highlight achievements that will benefit the employer. Describe how your work has led to measurable outcomes benefiting your organisation.
- **Is it easy to follow?**
  Keep to a logical pattern, following conventions. With a chronological CV, start with the most recent job and work backwards. Use present tense verbs for your current job, and past tense verbs for all previous jobs.
- **Are all the words used in their simplest form?**
  You don't want to make the person doing the shortlisting feel inferior if they don't understand your superabundance of polysyllabic terminology (your use of too many big words!).
- **Is it achievement-orientated?**
  As opposed to a list of what the job involved.

- **Are the verbs in the 'active' voice?**
  Write 'I did', 'I achieved' rather than, for example, 'I was recognised for'. Active: 'Delivered excellent customer service, leading to company recognition.' Passive: 'Was recognised for customer-service skills.'
- **Is what you have done quantified where appropriate?**
  Interviewers love the use of numbers, e.g. 'How much money/time did you save?'
- **Have you included your LinkedIn URL?**
  Jobvite's recruiting survey has identified that 93% of recruiters will look at a candidate's social presence, especially LinkedIn.
- **Have you read and read again?**
  You must re-read your CV – read for accuracy (numbers, city names, etc.), for missing/extra words, and then finally for spelling. Don't rely too heavily on a spellchecker; it will not catch misused yet properly spelled words like sun or son, site or sight, form or from, etc.
- **Is your CV free of jargon?**
  We often use abbreviations and acronyms (TOM, ALS, BPR), or internal descriptions for job roles which have little meaning for others. Make sure everything is easy to follow and ask someone else to read your CV to check they understand it.
- **Are you telling them only what they need to know?**
  Make sure it is concise and focused on the job you want.

Review the layout

It is usually best to stick to the following principles.

- **Margins should be at least one inch wide.** Don't make smaller margins so you can fit in more words. Edit instead.
- **Use bold formatting** for your name and section headings and to emphasise key words.
- **Use italics** for the names of publications and foreign phrases, if any.
- **Use just two font sizes**, and avoid ALL CAPS and too much underlining.
- **Do not justify the text**. A ragged right edge is much easier to read.
- **Put your name in the footer** using a smaller typeface.
- **Put the dates on the right-hand side** if you want to de-emphasise them.
- **Make all headings centred**. Research from The Ladders shows that a recruiter's eyes are drawn to the headers and then down the centre of the page.

IN A NUTSHELL

Your CV should now be looking much better. You have it focused on making an instant impact, holding key words and being ready for use by ATS software. You've chosen the most relevant style of CV and everything is focused on the job you seek.

BEFORE YOU MOVE ON

- Make a note of three key points you have learnt.
- Make a note of what is the top takeaway, for you, from this chapter.

- **Will you now revise your CV?**

9 LINKEDIN AND SOCIAL MEDIA

LinkedIn is helpful for finding jobs to apply for and it's useful for being found by recruiters.

This chapter will:

- talk you through what you need to have an effective LinkedIn presence

- explain how to use LinkedIn to raise your profile

- introduce you to some of the other social media you may like to consider.

Companies use social media, that's why ads are targeted to us online. Whether it's shoes or a holiday, Google knows what we want and keeps posting ads to encourage us to buy. The new way to look for jobs is via social media, both for research and to create a social presence that encourages organisations to want us to work for them.

The importance of social media

Many recruiters and employers will search for people on LinkedIn and it's a great source for jobs. They place ads on LinkedIn, use LinkedIn to find potential candidates and use the people they know, such as employees, to identify potentially strong hirees.

LinkedIn

With over 19 million people on LinkedIn in the UK and well over 400 million worldwide (January 2016), it's the place to be found, but it is also a giant search engine and can be an effective part of researching and networking.

To use it effectively, you must have a completed profile, with photo, recommendations and connections. Too many people leave their profile half-finished, without a photo, and then wonder why they don't have much success. That's like submitting a half-completed CV for a job and then wondering why you haven't been shortlisted. Or joining a gym and wondering why you haven't got any fitter – you need to do the work!

More and more recruiters fill the vacancies through social media that they haven't filled through referrals. An effective profile also allows you to connect with other people who work in the field you want to work in. You can ask questions, exchange information and find out about opportunities.

Be prepared

Without LinkedIn you will come across as unprepared; recruiters expect you to be on LinkedIn and this combines networking (the old) and social media (the new). It also allows you to be found.

Many times after you apply for a job and before you're invited to interview, the hiring manager will look you up on LinkedIn, so it acts like a first interview. First they check your picture, then read your headline – does it grab their attention? Only then will they skim your profile, including your recommendations.

How recruiters use LinkedIn

LinkedIn is a cost-effective way for recruiters to find people. They will enter their criteria, such as employee relations manager within a 25-mile radius of Chester with experience working for retail companies. If you meet these criteria, you will appear in their shortlist. Without a photo they'll probably move on and won't even review your profile. Otherwise, they'll do a quick review, paying attention to any recommendations you have. Recruiters also search for specific skills, so include the same relevant skills listed on your CV, and also get endorsements from people who recognise your skills.

LinkedIn is used by 93% of recruiters to identify candidates and 78% of companies have hired through social media (source Jobvite 2014), but in general people of 55+ are much less likely to use social media.

Case Study

Nilesh was delighted that revisions to his LinkedIn profile led to several contacts from recruiters.

Getting started

If you have an account, you can review everything as I talk you through this chapter. If this is new for you, this will provide the information you need.

You set up an account at linkedin.com which provides helpful guidance. First add some basic details: current situation, company, job title and postcode.

You will be asked to connect your email account to start connecting with people. I strongly recommend that you skip this step, and wait until you have got your profile completed – you don't want people coming to your profile when there is hardly any information entered.

If you need more detailed support **my eBook – *How to use LinkedIn to find a New Job***, available from www.amazingpeople.co.uk – guides you through all the steps in great detail.

The professional headline

You have 120 characters to create a professional headline, so make good use of them. This professional headline will be included each time you appear on LinkedIn. It appears as a status update, and also when you make a comment in a group, so you want it to stand out.

There are many ways you can write your headline, and you can change it whenever you like. You could say something as short as 'Management Accountant' but would that capture the attention of a recruiter? Think of the difference if you wrote something like, *'I save money for professional services firms by reviewing and improving processes.'*

As LinkedIn is being used more and more as a search engine, you may prefer to use a list of key words to increase your chances of being found through a search. Mine, using 120 characters, is:

Award Winning Career Coach | Author | Career Coaching | Job Search | LinkedIn Profile Makeovers | Personal Branding

Valerie had a very brief LinkedIn presence and with only five contacts she clearly wasn't making much use of it. Her professional headline was:

Unemployed and Looking for Work

This would not help her to get found – what recruiter will search for 'Unemployed' or 'Looking for Work'? There are two alternatives that would be better. The first is to make it key-word rich such as:

Award-winning Director | Producer | Scriptwriter | TV | Video Production | Editing | Final cut Pro | Post Production

Which comes in at 116 characters, out of a maximum of 120. This style will help you increase your ranking in search engines but it doesn't really convince the reader to review your profile. You may therefore prefer to take the time to work on a different style – to make a statement such as:

I love making awesome films and help others do that too! I produce scripts that make stylish, effective films

Photo

Upload a photo. Without one you will significantly reduce your chances of people connecting with you. Critically review the photos you have and choose a professional, head-and-shoulders shot, where people get a good view of your face and especially your eyes. Aim to smile and look approachable. It doesn't need to have been taken by a professional. Ask a friend to take a good number, make sure you have an uncluttered background and one is likely to be good.

Valerie's photo was almost full-length and taken from a great distance. It really wasn't helping.

Your LinkedIn profile is different to your CV, but the message should be consistent. Include highlights from your career history and also strengths you can offer an employer. You have key words in your CV; use these same key words in your LinkedIn profile to help with getting on a shortlist when employers are searching for people with a particular skill set.

On LinkedIn, we aren't constrained by a two-page layout and can write up our background and desires in a more market-focused way. The main objective should be to make it compelling.

Summary

You have up to 2,000 characters for your summary. What you write should be clear, focused on your objective and should take about 30 seconds to read out loud. Write in the first person. It should come across as if you are talking to the reader – imagine we are having a coffee together and you are telling me about yourself. You can use paragraphs and symbols such as ~~ or ** to break up the text.

If you plan to have a portfolio career or can't decide where to focus, you can include two sections within this summary, each focused on a different area.

Career history

In most cases it's best to write up your current job in paragraphs, again in a chatty style. Include key words and focus on value. What would make someone want to connect or get in touch? Put some effort into this section. You can look at other people for pointers and inspiration but don't copy.

Using key words in a LinkedIn profile

Use the key words you identified and include them throughout your profile; in particular make sure to include them in your headline, the summary, education, your most recent experience and, of course, in your skills.

Headline areas, like the job title, are considered more important than body text in the eyes of the search engine. However, if you can't fit a key word into a headline area, just use it in the body or description area.

If you don't have a degree – when I was 16 most of the pupils at my school were in our first jobs at this age – you can include 'degree calibre' or similar to get around the software that seeks to check you have a degree.

If you have a long work history and you are concerned that you might appear overqualified, only include the last 10–15 years of your job history, don't include the years when you were at university and focus more on your passion for the job, especially in your headline and the summary section.

Again, include key words and avoid company acronyms that lack meaning to others. You don't need to include every job; just like on your CV you can group short-term assignments together and you don't need to go back to your very first job.

Additional information

There are many optional sections. You don't need to include them all now, and not all will be relevant to you. The one area to focus on is the link to three websites. You don't need to use all three but this is the only place to include a hyperlink so it's well worth using if you can. If you have had an article published you could add a link to this. Most people use the default 'My Blog' or 'My Website' but you can change these to include the actual name of your blog or a more accurate description, such as 'My article on Career Development published in *People Management*' or 'Denise Taylor's personal website'. If you have a Twitter account you can include a link to your Twitter page.

Claim your name!

The default URL is a less-than-memorable mix of numbers and letters. This is very difficult for you and others to remember. But you may be able to use your name. Whilst mine is quite a common name, I was able to get http://uk.linkedin.com/in/denisetaylor. If this hadn't been available I would have included my middle initial or perhaps added MBA after my name.

You do this by choosing 'edit profile', then follow the hyperlink which will take you to a section describing how to change your profile URL. If you can't get your name because it has already been taken, they will make three suggestions, but you can also choose your own.

Location

Include the location where you want to work if you are considering a move, and include the postcode of e.g. central Manchester. Anita changed her location from Bournemouth to Chester as she was moving to be nearer her daughter.

Privacy settings

Check and make sure you are comfortable with your privacy settings. You do this via the 'account and settings' tab at the top of your profile. Make sure that your 'public profile' is set to display full profile information so that it's accessible to search engines. You can choose, for example, not to have your data shared with third-party applications, and whether you want advertising messages to be sent to you.

Turn off your activity broadcast, if currently employed, so your current boss doesn't see that you have now connected to 10+ recruiters and are following a competitor.

Seeking groups

There are over 500,000 groups on LinkedIn. Search for those that relate to your company, industry, school or career interests. You can join a maximum of 50 groups and this is a great way to make contacts and develop relationships. It's difficult to deal with the sheer number of updates for a large number of groups but you can opt for a daily or weekly digest or a 'no email' option. A benefit of joining a number of groups is that it increases the number of people you are connected with.

Find groups by putting key words into a search and see the ones that are most active, and which have the most members. Look at the conversations, unless it's a closed group.

Groups include:

- industry-specific groups
- trade and professional groups
- employer alumni groups
- career-related groups
- functional groups
- personal interest groups.

Start with just two groups that you will get involved with on at least a weekly basis – better to start small and build up than to get overwhelmed. Joining a group is not the same as participating – you must get involved to really get the benefit.

Before joining a group, review the group's statistics – member demographics, growth and activity – you don't want to join a group with little discussion. You can access this material via the 'i' icon on each group profile. Before joining, check out how active the group is. Ideally you want active groups with a lot of members.

Each group will operate slightly differently: some will automatically grant you access; with others, your application will be reviewed. Each group includes links to discussions, news, jobs and sometimes subgroups.

Groups are a great place to ask questions but also answer questions and respond to posts. This will raise your profile. Participate in discussions so people become familiar with your name and may seek you out.

You can only send a message to people you are connected with unless you pay to send an InMail. But if the person you want to contact belongs to the same group, you can generally message them. Find them through a search for members of the particular group.

Status update box
This allows you to provide details of what you are working on: for example, an event you are presenting at or attending, a significant accomplishment at work, a blog post or article you have published. Aim to update at least a couple of times a week.

Use status updates on your social media profiles to inform your network of your professional developments. List what conferences you are attending, what recent education initiatives you have undertaken and what new milestones you have achieved.

You also read other people's updates in your feed. If someone is over-sharing and you don't want to see these updates but you want to stay connected just scroll to the top right-hand corner the next time you see an update and click on the word 'hide'.

Getting ready to connect

You need to get the basics ready before attempting to connect with people – you want to come across as efficient (I would expect!) and interesting, so use this checklist of 12 pointers.

1. Is your profile focused on the sort of job you are looking for?
2. Have you identified and included relevant key words for this job in your tagline/summary/specialities?
3. Have you included your location?
4. Do you have a compelling headline? Don't copy someone else's; make it personal.
5. Do you have a professional photo that focuses on your head and shoulders? People want to be able to see your eyes!
6. Have you personalised your URL to make it easier to pass on details to others? You can then include this on your CV and in your email signature.
7. Is your summary compelling and easy to read? Does it showcase your key achievements? Would *you* want to get in touch with you?
8. Have you included details on your current and past experience? Include at least a short summary of each job. A recruiter may want to meet someone who has worked for a particular organisation, so be sure to name them.
9. Have you added top skills? You can include up to 50 skills.
10. Have you included education, projects, courses, etc.?
11. Do you have recommendations? Start by giving them to other people, people may then recommend you.
12. Have you joined relevant groups? Join groups which are relevant to what you are looking for. Where do the key players for your profession hang out?

Seeking connections

You are now ready to connect with people. You can search your email account and connect with people you know. Avoid sending out the default message. Instead choose a personal message that demonstrates some thought – people are more likely to accept your connection.

The best connection requests will mention why you are reaching out to them, what you have in common, and why you think they're great. The key here is to show them you've done your homework and that you know who they are.

It shouldn't look like you're just blindly trying to connect with people. If you struggle to write why you think they're interesting then you either haven't done enough research yet or it's simply not someone you should connect with.

Search for people you used to work with or met at school or university; it might be interesting to see what they are doing now. You can also look through the collection of business cards you have accumulated and connect with people who gave their cards to you.

You will see a list of people that you may like to connect with. Click the tick on your mobile or tablet and the generic message is sent – you don't get the option to add a message. Better to send from your laptop or PC where you can include a personal message. Something like this:

> *Hi Matt, you've just popped up as someone I might know. I don't know you yet, but you have an interesting background and I'd be happy to connect if you wanted to. Best wishes, Denise Taylor*

You are welcome to connect with me on LinkedIn – https://uk.linkedin.com/in/denisetaylor.

Case Study

Suzanne said: 'As someone over 50 who has previously made a career change I'm not afraid of adapting as necessary in order to find work. In particular I'm aware that I need to learn more about using technology both inside and outside the classroom. I'm also intending to create a new LinkedIn profile for myself. I had one a few years ago when I was doing some coaching, but I removed it when I stopped doing coaching as I wasn't looking for clients or work. As I work out exactly what I'll be offering, in addition to teaching English as a foreign language, I'll create my LinkedIn profile and join groups as you've suggested.'

Building connections

Recruiters may make judgements depending on the number of connections you have on LinkedIn – the more connections, the more potential customers is a view in some industries.

Add recruiters to your network

Recruiters use LinkedIn Recruiter (a paid service) which means that they can see candidate information in a different way to us. They can't see every person on LinkedIn, they still only see the details of people with whom they are connected, so having a connection with them increases your chance of being contacted. Recruiters want you in their network because they may want to pitch you for a position. So they are very likely to accept your connection invite. They only have a limited number of free connections, so are careful with how many of these free connections they use each month.

The more recruiters you have in your network, the greater your chance of helpful second-degree connections and of appearing in search results.

A further benefit is that external recruiters work with companies, so when you add a recruiter as a primary contact, you may well then have second-level contacts (people your contacts know) working for the company that you would like to work for.

Once you have connected with the people you already know, you can seek to connect with second-level contacts. Aim to get your contacts up to 150–200 in the next few weeks, then build on from there. More people need to know you exist.

You must build real connections, and not just collect connections. I get in touch with all my contacts a couple of times a year. Around 18% reply, enough to make me feel it is worthwhile.

Recommendations and endorsements

People pay attention to recommendations, and you should seek these from people you have worked with in the past. You could tell them the sort of job you are looking for and your key attributes, skills and achievements, so they can write with this in mind. Recommendations don't have to be long, and you may find that past bosses and colleagues are happy to provide one.

If it has been a while, you could remind them of your achievements and personal qualities. Sometimes people are just so busy so you could draft something for them to edit.

If you are being made redundant, ask your manager for a recommendation before you leave. The recommendation will let other people know that you were valued. You could also seek recommendations from clients if you are connected to them. As the manager, you can also ask for a recommendation from your team, possibly focused on your leadership qualities.

Also recommend others – be specific in what you say. Your recommendation will then appear on both your profile and theirs.

Skills endorsements

Most people spend only a few minutes looking at your profile. As they skim your profile, the list of skills is an easy way to quickly assess your expertise. To begin, list your skills from the 'edit profile' option. Click 'edit' in the skills section and start typing in the skills you already have listed on your CV. As you type, other options will appear; decide if you want to include these.

If you already have skills listed, go through and take out any that are irrelevant for the job you seek. You click 'X' to the right of the skill. Make sure you include variations of a skill, as sometimes people will search using a slightly different term.

You can also rearrange the skills and put the most important ones first. You are more likely to get endorsed for the skills at the top. If you think you may have missed skills, you can review the profiles of people who work in a similar job to yours (or the one you seek).

Research and networking on LinkedIn

Use LinkedIn to build connections with the company you want to work for. Ask to connect with the people who would be your peers and managers. Look at the LinkedIn groups they belong to, join and get involved in discussions. Joining is not enough; you need to be an active participant. Raise your profile by answering questions, or share information by posting links to articles, with a reason why others should read them. You could also see if potentially important connections have a Twitter handle and follow them, or get an introduction through someone you know.

If you want to apply for a job within a particular company but don't know who to contact, you need to find someone who can help you. You can use LinkedIn to find people who work, or have worked, for a particular company and send them a message. It doesn't even have to be someone in the department you want to work in – often contacting someone from a different department can be just as useful. For example, if you are an electrical engineer, you can make contact with an accountant at that company and ask them questions. Here are some suggestions of how to make that first contact.

- *'I'm really interested in working with XYZ Company as an electrical engineer. Would you be able to suggest the right person for me to talk with?'*
- *'As someone who has worked with XYZ Company for four years, can you suggest ways I could make a speculative application stand out from many others?'*
- *'I have an interview scheduled next week with XYZ Company – could you let me know more about what it's like to work with your company and, in particular, details about the company culture?'*

You can use LinkedIn to research people doing the job you want – look at their profiles to see what certifications and specific experience they have. You may see that people in the jobs you aspire to all belong to a specific professional association; if so, join a relevant LinkedIn group.

Look up people who work for the organisation that interests you and note where they previously worked. You could also look up people who have moved on from that organisation, and find out where they moved to – it could provide interesting career paths to review.

You may feel uncomfortable making contact with someone currently working for the organisation and who you barely know; you may prefer to contact ex-employees. They also may be more willing to talk openly about what it is really like to work there.

LinkedIn allows you to save up to ten job searches and three people searches. After conducting a search, click on the 'save search' option on the right to allow you to run this search again. You also have the option to receive weekly or monthly reminders via email once new members of your network or new jobs match your saved search criteria.

Introductions

You may be very keen to contact someone who is not part of your network. If that person is connected to someone you know, you can ask them to introduce you. However, just because a person is a first-level contact with someone, it doesn't mean that they know them well, so if they decline to help, it's probably not down to anything you have done.

When asking for an introduction, create a short email that they can then send on to the person you want to connect with. Write it as if it is from them, so that the changes they need to make are minimal. Draw out your achievements and include details to make somebody feel compelled to connect to you.

You can also use InMail. If you have opted for the premium (paid) service you can send messages to anyone, whether you are connected or not.

Move connections offline

LinkedIn is not just about numbers of contacts but what you do with them. You can arrange to meet in person or to set up a Skype meeting if you live some distance away.

Make LinkedIn part of a weekly routine

You can't complete your profile and think that's it! At least a couple of times a week, update your status, read updates from your connections, read and comment on discussions within groups you belong to, review your connections, see what they are doing and how you can help, identify jobs to apply for, and use LinkedIn to help with research. Review too your descriptions and list of skills in case changes would be beneficial.

As a job-seeker, look at the message featuring jobs LinkedIn have identified for you based on your profile, but also be proactive. You will find jobs through using the search function and also by checking the job tab of the groups you belong to.

Grow your contacts

Read again the earlier section on joining groups. You want to be found, so join some of the groups with the largest number of members. TopLink will list all the groups; you could join the top 50 and get a huge number of connections but you still want to make sure your connections are in areas where you want to get involved. www.toplinked.com helps you build larger, more diverse and more valuable networks on the world's top social-networking sites.

Publishing on LinkedIn

Alongside your status updates you can also create blog posts that have the potential to reach a good number of members. The best way to get more people to read your post is to choose a good heading, and do some publicity. But don't annoy group members by self-promotion, rather include a discussion point.

The paid service

The free service should be enough. Think carefully before you spend your money on the paid service unless you can see clear benefits.

Using LinkedIn as part of your direct-approach strategy

Some companies will accept a LinkedIn invitation but not an unsolicited CV, so as you identify organisations that you are interested in working for, follow them. Join groups where the employees belong and send a personalised email to relevant members of staff – not HR, but the person you would work for, or with, if you joined the organisation.

It's your data

You can now request a zip file of your LinkedIn data. This includes a complete list of your first-level connections, your search history and more. You access this by going to your photo on the top right of your tool bar, select 'privacy and settings', choose 'account' and then choose 'request an archive of your data', which you will get within 72 hours. Mine arrived in less than 12 hours.

What about other social media?

I've concentrated on LinkedIn as this is the most important social media site to use.

LinkedIn is excellent if you are looking for a job in the UK or USA. There are other social media sites such as Xing, used extensively in Germany, so if you are looking to work overseas, do check on the most valuable resources for a particular country.

You could also consider Twitter, Facebook and Google+.

Twitter

Twitter is increasingly being used by employers to advertise job opportunities. For example RBS and Deloitte have set up special Twitter streams for jobs.

You don't need to be active, but it is useful to connect with organisations that you want to work for. You can use search.twitter.com to develop a list of job-search leads. You can also participate in Twitter job chats such as #jobhuntchat and #LinkedInChat.

To add some content to your stream you can add links to any interesting articles you find and RT (retweet) interesting items in your feed. When you do post any link, due to the limited number of characters available, use TinyURL, for example, to shorten the link.

Facebook

If you have a Facebook account you can use BranchOut to utilise your Facebook network to find your inside connections. You can search for a person, company, or job title. To trial this, I typed in UCAS, a local company, and found that I have two second-level connections – friends of friends.

I could put in a friend request or ask our friend-in-common to make an introduction.

Using BeKnown, part of Monster, means that when you get your job-search results from Monster you will also see who you know at each company. You can also share your Monster profile with employers so they can see your professional achievements and experience.

Google+

Google+ is reportedly bigger than LinkedIn with 600M+ users, so if you are using social media it will help to set up an account and to also include posts and comments from other social media sites here. As Google+ is part of Google, comments here help to raise your profile through your Google rankings.

Social job search

Jackalope Jobs allows you to use your social connections. The website says: 'We search your social profiles and those of your connections to provide the right openings and right connections that can help you land your dream job. Your connections through multiple social networks now can help you in your job search.'

IN A NUTSHELL

You should now feel much happier with your LinkedIn presence, and it should read well when compared to your CV. But this isn't done and dusted! You need to be an active LinkedIn user, so make sure you get involved in groups and create regular status updates. Perhaps diarise to go on this site for 30–45 minutes twice a week to raise your profile and look for jobs to apply for.

BEFORE YOU MOVE ON

- Make a note of three key points you have learnt.
- Make a note of what is the top takeaway, for you, from this chapter.

- **Will you now revise your LinkedIn profile?**

10 PROMOTING YOURSELF AND BEING FOUND

You now have your CV and LinkedIn profile. Both will be excellent for your job search. You also need to go a bit further and make sure that you are found.

In this chapter, we:

- explain why you also need to consider your voicemail message, email signature and business cards

- discuss why you may need more than one CV

- suggest that you can get known through preparing a presentation and a special report

- discuss the six ways you can grow your online presence

- remind you that anything you write online can be picked up by search engines, and the need to set up alerts.

To increase your chance of success you need to promote yourself, both when you meet with people and also online. And to do that you need a consistent message and a variety of 'marketing' materials.

Being found

Many people I talk with are proud that they can't be found online but you need an online presence so that potential employers who check you out before shortlisting find **you**, and definitely not negative material on someone who shares your name.

What will be found if someone else looks for you online? Alongside a standard search you can also google your name in Google images to see what pictures of you can be found on the web.

A consistent message

Voicemail message

You don't want to be caught off guard when a recruiter calls you for an impromptu phone interview, so don't dash to answer the phone. Let your professional voice message take the call and call back when the time is right for you. You will need a personalised message, don't just insert your name into the automated voicemail greeting.

Phone your mobile and listen to the message. Be critical. What impression does it give? Do you sound upbeat and professional? Is there any distracting background noise? Is it too long? Make it short, something like:

> *Thanks for calling Denise Taylor. I'm unavailable at this time. Leave a message and I'll call you back as soon as I can, and thanks for calling.*

And make sure it shows some energy – have your voice rise a little at the end. It can help to record this and make all phone conversations standing up.

Email signature

The most important information to include is your name, phone number, email address, desired occupation and link to your LinkedIn profile alongside your tagline and a key question to get the reader interested. An easy solution is to use an app like WiseStamp to create and insert your signature.

Denise Taylor of Amazing People
Chartered Psychologist, Award Winning Career Coach and Author, I help clients get clarity on who they are, what they want to do and be successful in job search.
01684 772888 || 07931 303367 || denise@amazingpeople.co.uk
http://www.amazingpeople.co.uk

Business cards

Whilst you can get very low-cost ones, these often have their marketing logo on the back. You may prefer the more stylish cards available from Moo cards – http://uk.moo.com.

More than one CV

Your CV is likely to be a couple of pages in length and will be highly targeted to the specific job you seek. It also helps to have an extended master CV which contains full examples from every job, so that you can pull out the most relevant ones for the job you seek and create a targeted CV. You may also like to create the following materials.

A one-page marketing document

Yes, you have a CV, but will that be enough to grab the attention of your target audience? It's useful to have a one-page document that's a combination of a marketing document and a sales pitch. It focuses on key accomplishments and may include images, but most importantly it makes someone want to get in touch.

Focus it 100% on the position you seek; nothing is generic, nothing is left to chance, and everything is there to make a point. State brief teaser details, enticing the reader to pick up the phone and call you. Remember though, you must have the facts to back up your claims once you meet.

Include short paragraphs on your key accomplishments, special skills, career history and education, and something that bit different! Within this, include some pertinent quotes from former employers, clients, customers, etc. You want the person who receives this to be so impressed that they pick up the phone to call you.

I think these documents look best when the text is kept to one side, stylishly designed with key information set out in paragraphs. Good use is made of white space. A single-page document can be helpful when you are making a direct approach, or it could be a 'leave behind' document after a first interview. Make sure to include working links to online profiles.

A portfolio

You could create a folder of key examples of your work; have this ready to share with people you meet. This is a portfolio of your achievements. It can include articles, testimonials, certificates, and plans, all supported by charts, graphs and other visual images. Take it along when you meet people and use it to talk through your strengths. Create a master folder of everything that might be relevant and then re-order it for relevance before a meeting.

A visual CV

A typical CV is static, a visual CV is interactive, found online and demonstrates that you are 'tech savvy'. It's the proof that you understand new technology. It's not just you describing your excellent presentational skills – you can link to a video hosted on YouTube or Vimeo or create an audio so a potential employer can hear your passion for your subject.

A video CV

Companies are now offering the service for you to have a video CV. My main concern about a video CV is that it takes much longer for a recruiter to watch than the cursory scan given to a printed CV, but it could be useful once a shortlist has been created.

Talks and presentations

You could create talks lasting 15 minutes or longer on an area of expertise. Initially you could do these for free. Find out who to contact through searching for local organisations that want speakers. You could also offer to talk to local colleges and universities.

Prepare a presentation

Prepare a 15–20-minute presentation which shows how you can contribute to the profitability of the company. Think about three problems the employer has, and present a plan for how you would solve these. You don't need to go into too much detail, but you need to demonstrate that you understand the problems and know how to address them. Then directly contact the company to schedule a meeting to discuss.

Create a special report (white paper)

A great way to be seen as an expert is to create a special report. This can be an analysis of your industry or sector and demonstrates your knowledge of this area. It can also enhance your credibility if you are looking to move into a new sector. Special reports can be summaries of best practice or something topical. They can end with a call to action – the offer of further discussion or more information if requested. Of course, it should also have links to all your online profiles.

To create your report you could contact key people working in the particular sector. For people who don't like cold-calling, this approach provides a purpose to the call. You are calling to seek information and you will be able to follow up with the person you spoke with when you send them a copy of your report.

Once created, you can include your special report on your CV and have it available as a download via your LinkedIn page. You can also use it to create an article or series of articles that are posted on article hub sites, and perhaps use this as the basis for a presentation that you include on SlideShare.

Growing your online presence

The best way of being found is through an effective LinkedIn profile. You can also grow your online presence and build (or validate) your credibility by sharing your knowledge on key topics within your expertise.

Many jobs are highly competitive and you will want to take action to raise your profile. You need to develop marketing material which is focused on the job you want and why you should get the job.

Many people are reticent about sharing their success. You've got to get past this. You need to let other people know about your success. LinkedIn is a good choice but there are plenty more places where you could be found. You don't need to choose all of them, but read on and decide where you should focus some of your energy. You may like to consider the following six options.

1. Video (YouTube or Vimeo)

If you are comfortable in front of a camera, you could create a short YouTube video to demonstrate your speaking abilities – useful if you are e.g. seeking work as a trainer, or to discuss your passion for the job. Make sure you look good, and practise looking straight at the lens. It doesn't have to be long, just one minute can get your passion and enthusiasm across. If you like this, you could create your own YouTube channel and regularly include new videos.

2. Online presentation (SlideShare)

Create, or take a PowerPoint presentation – this can include samples of your work and images – and add some narration to bring it to life. Upload your presentation to SlideShare, which in 2016 was getting 70 million unique visitors a month.

3. Personal website or blog

A work-focused website could include a number of pages to expand on your CV. You could include more detail on your skills and experience and copies of presentations you have made, pictures of you at work, any articles you have written, etc. You can also include non-work-related activity that could be useful, such as community involvement and independent travel.

A personal website, where you comment on current issues facing your industry, can introduce you as an expert on the subject. Blogs can be included in newsfeeds and can quickly get picked up. Someone I know who is a stress-management expert commented on the link between diet and stress, based on something she read in the paper, and found herself at the top of Google for that particular search term.

A low-cost way to set up a website is to use a service such as Weebly.com.

Useful pages to include are:

- Who am I?/Bio
- Strengths

- Work Experience
- Passions
- Examples.

An alternative to a website is a blog. It can showcase your work – examples of designs or articles. You must keep a blog current, so at least once a week make an entry such as commenting on articles, news and your opinion on work-related topics. Blog posts can be your thoughts on industry topics, reviews of books or stories of the people you want to help, for example. You can also interview thought leaders and then create an article. Phoning someone up to ask to interview them is an effective way of building a connection. You could even document your job search.

Don't worry if you don't have the technical skills to create a website. You can find a freelancer on Elance or similar and get one set up for around £100. An alternative is to use a free service such as www.wix.com.

For a blog you will want:

- **a homepage** that clearly explains who you are and what you do
- **an About page** with your brief bio. Include a link to your LinkedIn profile
- **a Contact page** that lists your email address and other ways to connect with you.

Focus on shorter posts, under 800 words rather than long essays, and break it up into small paragraphs. Photos enhance text and make it more appealing.

If you start a blog, you need to keep it up to date, and if it focuses on job-hunting rather than raising your profile, be sure to clear it once you have a job. You don't want your new employer to think you are already looking for another job.

You can also turn blog posts into articles and upload them on article hub sites such as HubPages. These can have links back to your website or blog.

Then, **let people know** that you have created a blog or website, and be sure to include details on your CV and applications.

4. Writing articles

You could write articles and submit them to publications read by your target employer, blogs, magazines and online journals, and especially consider your professional journal. Focus on key words that people will search for. Also think about the headline – would it make you want to read it?

Many professional associations have journals and newsletters, and many companies have in-house magazines. To find out about publication details, contact the editor so you are clear on the typical length for such an article, how the article should be submitted, etc. You could also submit an article to an article hub such as ezinearticles.com. If you are going to submit articles, you can create a bio with brief details on your background. Base your bio on your marketing message and make sure to include a link to a website or your LinkedIn profile.

Writing an article can get you access to people who are otherwise unavailable. When making a cold call to ask about a job, it can be difficult to get through. However, phoning someone and saying, *'Hello! This is Jo Harvey and I'm writing an article on the current challenges in charity marketing. May I please talk with your chief executive?'* stands a much better chance of success. This could then prove very helpful when you go for interview at a charity marketing department.

Once you have an article printed, arrange for reprints so you can enclose them with your CV or direct-approach letters.

You could also create a special report based on some industry research that you could use, both on your blog and to send out. **All of these can be added to your LinkedIn profile.**

5. Comment on other people's blogs

You could read other people's blogs and make comments. Comments don't have to be long – just one or two paragraphs will be fine. If you're not sure what people in your industry are reading, search on alltop.com. Use the alphabetical directory on the top search bar to find blogs in your field. Your comments, signed with your name, will create links back to your own blog and will also get your name picked up by search engines.

6. Write Amazon reviews of books in your field

As you seek a new job, you can spend some of your free time reading relevant business books and write reviews on Amazon. This would be a good example of keeping up to date and is a great way to be thought of as knowledgeable. These reviews will also be picked up on search engines and will help to raise your profile. Use your full name.

Keeping track of your name in the online news

Anything you write online should get picked up by search engines. If you have a Google account, you can set up alerts for both your name and key words on companies that interest you.

IN A NUTSHELL

This chapter was about promoting yourself and being found. We've covered the need for a consistent message, why you may need more than one CV, and various ideas to promote yourself.

ACTIVITY 29

BEFORE YOU MOVE ON

- Make a note of three key points you have learnt.
- Make a note of what is the top takeaway, for you, from this chapter.

- **How are you going to raise your reputation?**
- **Which is your favourite method for raising your online profile?**

11 TAKING A DIRECT APPROACH

There are different ways to get a job; you can be reactive or proactive. The reactive approach is to respond to job advertisements – more details in the next chapter. The proactive approach is to take charge of how your job search develops.

Being proactive includes both contacting companies direct or through people you know – your contacts. This means you need to expand your personal and professional networks.

In this chapter you will learn:

- why you should use the direct approach, a process that takes you from initial research, through making contact to meeting success

- an alternative approach – knock on doors

- why it doesn't have to be a full-time job.

Taking a direct approach will work for people at all levels, from those in low-skilled work to senior professionals. I will talk you through what to do – so read on and take action.

Introducing the direct approach

Around 70% of jobs are found through the hidden job market (networking and direct approaches), but only 30% of people use this method. Most find it easier to apply for jobs even when it doesn't work.

You can wait for jobs to be advertised but you can also make a direct approach to the hiring manager within the organisations that you want to work for. You contact the person who would be your manager, not HR, unless you want to work in HR.

Many of my clients tell me this direct approach is not for them, it hasn't worked. But the approach they have taken has been to mailshot their CV with a bland and ill-focused cover letter. Yes, that approach doesn't work. What I suggest is much more likely to succeed.

This direct approach may well take you outside your comfort zone, but if what you are doing hasn't worked, you need to try something new – connect with a relevant person within an organisation, someone who may have the power to give you a job or to help you on your way to the job you seek.

Having a great CV and an effective LinkedIn profile is essential. You also need to understand the process. Look at this image:

Ideal role
3 offers
5 final stage interviews
8 first-stage interviews
15 potential career opportunities
30 half-hour conversations
50 short (10–15 minute) conversations
Identify key decision-makers – link to them on LinkedIn
Identify key sectors for the job you seek

You can see that you start broad, have conversations and eventually get a job offer for the job you want.

Rachael hadn't really considered this as an approach that would work for her, and Phil said that he had contacted a few people without success. Gary had sent out a mailshot but had never followed up. Richard thought an employer could see this as a bit sneaky, but it is through an initial conversation that both you and the person you meet will decide whether to take an initial enquiry further. So you need to be clear why you are getting in touch and find out areas where you can help and add value.

I reminded them why this approach works.

- Many jobs are going to be advertised and your letter arrives before the details have been finalised and the ad has been placed. This worked for Suzanne. Her letter arrived just as they were planning to start the process to recruit more staff.
- Some companies have a need for more people, but they haven't really thought through what they want the person to do, it's all a bit vague. A letter outlining how you can solve their problems will grab their attention and encourage them to meet you. This may lead to a job being created.
- Situations where an incumbent has privately made known to their manager their plans to leave, and this change has not been announced publicly. The manager wants to replace them and is quietly making known to others the need for a replacement. Your approach is at the right time.
- A position may be occupied by an incumbent and the company does not want to make a change until they have the 'right' candidate.
- The vacancy would have been filled by an internal candidate had you not written to the organisation at that time.

Jobs that are likely to be advertised can be found through people you know within the organisation, hence the need to connect a range of people – see Chapter 7.

The direct approach is not difficult, it just takes time to do it well. Enjoy the process. You are going to learn some practical skills, so read on.

How it works

Phil had only gained three interviews out of over 100 applications, so he knew the traditional approach wasn't working. Although initially dubious, after a discussion on the process he wrote seven letters. These could have been better-focused and didn't generate any interest. He then targeted his letter much more carefully, with greater attention to research. Each was sent to a named person and he followed up with a phone call requesting a short meeting. Out of six letters he got five positive responses. He met with three people – one offered consultancy work and another permanent work. Phil was very clear that his success was down to effective research and taking a direct approach. Richard said that when he'd used this approach back in 2007 to contact FTSE 100 firms he could have been clearer on what he had to offer and would now follow these steps.

Like Richard, you need to prepare thoroughly, and follow these steps.

Step 1:   Research (identify key sectors for the job you seek)

Step 2:   Connect (identify key decision-makers – link to them on LinkedIn)

Step 3:   Create your letters

Step 4:   Post your letters

Step 5:   Follow up with a phone call

Step 6:   Meetings

Step 7:   Next Steps

Research

You know your strengths and the type of job you want. Now identify the type of organisations which are likely to have a need for someone like you. You also need to be clear on location – there is little point approaching organisations based in London if you need to live in Bristol and the job isn't flexible.

Research will focus both on current issues that you can use to target an approach and also relevant companies.

You can identify organisations through:

■ suggestions from friends and colleagues
■ reading newspapers (including local) and the trade press and looking online to see which organisations are growing, who is gaining government tenders,

etc. You can also see which companies are advertising, maybe not in your field, but if they are taking on employees in one area, there may be other opportunities soon

■ attending professional meetings, conferences, networking events, classes or workshops

■ walking or driving around business and science parks to identify possible companies to approach

■ using LinkedIn's advanced search. From this, and taking account of location, you can identify around 15–20 organisations that you would like to work for.

Focus on different-sized organisations – many smaller organisations could also have a need for someone like you.

Deeper research.

As you identify organisations you can understand the sector challenges and any trends. Find these out via company websites, product reviews and news and press releases. Read their blogs, check them out on Twitter. Alongside a Google search you can also research them on glassdoor.com. See if you can identify any problems that you could solve. Find out more by following them on LinkedIn and Twitter and liking their Facebook page.

Instead of looking for a job, look for a company.

Who would you like to work for? How could you help them? The focus is on researching a company, identifying what they do and how you can help – acting like a consultant. Talk with people who work for this company, get them to know you and what you can offer and aim to be the person they will contact when they have a need for a problem-solver. More on this in Chapter 13, Alternatives to a permanent full-time job.

Find jobs through the business press.

Find out about an expanding company through reading the business press. You can also see which companies are advertising, maybe not in your field, but if they are taking on employees in one area, there may be other opportunities soon. Job advertisements are a useful source of intelligence for your job-search campaign.

Rethink your networking.

For many, networking is asking if people know of job openings. It should be focused on finding out how you can help a company. Talk to people about what you want to do, how you help organisations and seek help in making connections with people who work for a particular company. Your focus must be on being seen as an expert, not to come across as a job-hunter.

Connect

Before sending out your letters, set up fact-finding meetings for more research. There are lots of ways to find people and the more connections you have on LinkedIn, the easier it will be. Remember, these aren't just paper connections, you need to build relationships with them. Once you have decided which companies to contact, find out who you know already that works there. Is there someone on the inside who would recommend you; perhaps they could personally deliver your letter?

Leverage your network.

Go back to LinkedIn, use the company search capability and enter the name of the company that interests you. When the listing comes up it will tell you how many people in your network work there.

Use LinkedIn to identify who runs the relevant departments or who used to run them; ideally you want to **network with the people who used to work for these companies**. They will be more open to answering specific questions about the department, the company and the challenges. Tell them you are undertaking research.

Follow the organisations on LinkedIn.

You will see the names of people who are currently employed by the organisation. You can also run a search on a target company to get a list of employees, and can search for past team members to see where they are currently employed.

Connect with current employees by sending a personalised request, explain why you are interested in their company and include something of interest to them.

Ask to set up an informational/fact-finding meeting of about 20 minutes.
Don't ask about a job, concentrate on finding out more about them, their work, why they like the organisation, the problems the organisation faces and any advice they can offer.

Move beyond finding out about the type of work to understand the problems faced in this industry in general and this organisation in particular. You can then approach a hiring manager in one of the organisations that you want to work for and tell them you understand some of their problems, and can help. Suggest a meeting.

Identify who runs the department.
Now you have a list of organisations to contact, but who will you write to?
Not HR unless that's where you want to work. With smaller organisations it will be the managing director or owner. If you can't find the information online, phone up and ask the name of e.g. the marketing director or the operations manager.

It helps to build a referral network, hence the overlap with Chapter 7, Connecting with others.

Create your letters

You are not applying for a job so you won't be creating a typical cover letter. Instead you will let the reader know that you understand some of the issues that affect their organisation and some of the ways that you can help.

This cannot be a mailshot approach, or as with Gary and Rachael it will just lead to disappointment. You must target your letter to the particular organisation. You must demonstrate that you have taken time to understand more about the organisation, their problems and also the role of the person you are writing to. You do not focus on what you want – your goals and objectives – but on how you can help them. Your objective is to get a face-to-face interview. Do not include your CV and if you are out of work, don't mention this.

This is **a sales letter that emphasises accomplishments, not experiences**, and is probably one side and a maximum of two sides long.

If you are looking for work as a management accountant, there will be a lot of similarities between the letters you send to different organisations, but you still want a degree of personalisation and your letter will differ if you are applying to a firm of architects or a light engineering company.

The objective of the letter is not to get you a job but to get you seen by a decision-maker. Demonstrate that you understand the organisation's needs. Think about the problems that must be faced by the reader. How can your combination of experience, training and aptitude help to deal with them? How can you make their life easier or more profitable?

A benefit of being older is that generally our emails and letters will be well written. **Follow conventional business styling but make sure they are not too formal.** It's a more informal (but not sloppy) world. Richard said that this made sense to him.

This is a time-consuming approach, but you will have a much higher success rate if you tailor your letter specifically rather than take the mailshot approach.

Learn from Gary – his poorly targeted approach was not focused on what he could offer and is clearly a letter sent to many, setting him up for rejection. Here's how **not** to do it.

> *Dear Sir/Madam,*
>
> *I am writing to apply for a job as a testing manager. I have a total of 29 years' experience in this area.*
>
> *Attached is my detailed CV for your review. I would appreciate the opportunity to speak with a member of your recruiting team in due course.*
>
> *I can be reached anytime via email at XXXXXX@hotmail.com or 07801 5xxxxx*
>
> *Thank you very much for your consideration.*
>
> *Yours faithfully,*

Look at what's wrong with it – there's no recipient name, it asks for a job, he includes his (four-page) CV and is expecting them to contact him. Plus, it mentions 29 years! Fifteen-plus years would be enough, but do years of service make you want to get in touch with him? As a reader I would want to know how he can be of help to me.

Focus your letter 100% on the job you seek. Nothing is generic, nothing is left to chance. State teaser details to encourage them to pick up the phone and call you.

The key principles

Paragraph 1

Introduction – Start off with something that demonstrates you've done your research – perhaps they have gained a new contract or won an award. You can find this through a Google Alert or by looking at the news section of their website. Make them want to read on.

Or start with a catchy opening statement, about your passion for the subject or the particular organisation.

As a marketing manager for a leading consumer product, I helped increase sales by 13% through a new marketing policy.

You want to show quickly how you can benefit the organisation, so don't start with the word 'I'.

Paragraphs 2 and 3

How you can help – For example, you've found they have a new large contract, or won an award, and are likely to be busy or are losing market share, so you want to let them know that you know they need help (there has to be a reason to increase your chance of a positive reply). Make a connection between what you can offer and the needs of the organisation, for example:

Your company may be in need of a sales consultant. If so, you may be interested in what I have achieved in sales.

Or

If your company needs a manufacturing manager with my background and experience, you may be interested in some of the things I have done.

Or

Do you have a need for a marketing manager? You may be interested in some of my accomplishments . . .

Be clear why they should be interested in you – Provide strong evidence of relevant achievements and experience. It's great if you can include how you saved money, made money, solved a problem. You should have these examples on your CV and you can add more detail about your contribution. If possible, include numerical data to emphasise any achievements, just like on your CV.

You can mention your educational background, qualifications, etc. to add credibility to what you are saying. **Do not include anything which is not highly relevant for the job you seek**.

Paragraph 4

End your letter by saying what you will do next – Do not finish with something like 'I would appreciate an opportunity to discuss any openings that you may have in your organisation.' This weakens your position. You are selling yourself in your speciality.

Don't say that you will wait to hear from them, or you will be waiting forever. Far better to write something such as:

If you would like to discuss my experience in greater detail, I shall be glad to do so at a personal interview. I will phone you early next week.

Finally, learn from marketing people and include a PS. Perhaps something like:

If you've got a need for an additional resource and would love to know more about how I saved (the organisation) £xxx, I'd be very pleased to talk with you.

Once complete, read it out loud. Do the phrases come easily, or are the sentences so long that you run out of breath? Read it out loud to a friend or colleague and make sure they understand what you are trying to say.

EXAMPLE 1

Dear (name),

Please excuse my direct approach. I have been following (company name) for a while and in light of your company's recent announcement, I believe there is now a real opportunity for us to work together.

I have built my career on three pillars: increasing revenue, boosting performance and turning relationships around.

What differentiates me is my approach to doing this. I love a challenge, and I use all my creativity and analytical skills in solving problems and driving results.

This is how I increased monetisation by 14% and bookings by 25% at XXXX in 18 months, thus turning around revenue decline. It's also how I more than halved inventory days at XXXX in less than a year.

Would you be available for a quick phone call to explore your challenges and how I could best support you?

I'll give your assistant a call in the next few days to schedule a time to talk, or feel free to call me any time on 07931 356 xxx.

I am looking forward to hearing from you.

Best regards,

EXAMPLE 2

This was sent following seeing details of a new store coming to an out-of-town shopping centre.

> *Congratulations on opening a new branch of (company name). Expansion must be exciting and you must be keen to get staff with sufficient enthusiasm for both the product and the customer. It takes time to train new staff.*
>
> *When I was recruited for a new store opening I quickly got up to speed with the products, and soon became known as the 'go to' person for the other new staff. I also got great customer feedback, being seen as efficient and helpful.*
>
> *I'd love to bring my experience and knowledge to your new store. Feel free to contact me so we could discuss how I could help.*

Don't send your CV. Send only your letter – you want to grab their interest, and attaching a CV can direct your correspondence to HR.

EXAMPLE 3

Break my rules, this worked for Anita, I've said not to use a mailshot approach, but when you want another job that is very much like the job you are currently doing this approach can work.

Use your research to create a mailing list of at least 100 people who work in the type of organisation you seek. With Anita, this was law firms. Anita wanted to continue as a legal executive but in a new location, 150 miles away. Aim to send out around 20 letters a week, and keep sending them out even as you move into a second-interview phase. A job could fall through at the last stage and so you need to make sure that you won't have to start from scratch again.

> *Dear (name),*
>
> *I have been working for XXXX of (town/city) in their conveyancing department for the past nine years and have recently qualified as a Fellow of the Institute of Legal Executives.*

After 3 years as a paralegal I was promoted to a fee earner specialising in residential conveyancing.

I have worked in all branches of the firm and provided expert holiday cover for both solicitors and partners. I have acted for a number of high-profile clients as the partners of the firm have confidence in my abilities. The partners also gave me complicated transactions to deal with and I have received a number of thank-you letters from clients together with excellent client survey responses, examples of which I attach.

For personal reasons I intend to relocate to Chester and I'm looking to continue to work as a legal executive with a firm that wants someone focused on both customer care and business bottom-line profit.

Highlights from my CV include

X

X

X

I would be grateful if you could advise me of any opportunities you may have and I would be pleased to attend an interview at your convenience.

I look forward to hearing from you.

Yours faithfully,

Anita Watson Inst.L.Ex.

Encl: CV, sample letters of appreciation and client survey.

Post your letters

Whilst you could email I suggest you take a retro approach and send an actual letter, printed on good quality paper, signed with a good quality pen. It's so rare to get a business letter nowadays that your correspondence will get more attention and be much less likely to be discarded.

I also suggest that you hand-write the address, and possibly send it in a greetings-card envelope to increase the chance of it being opened.

Follow up with a phone call

Don't forget to add a reminder to your diary/calendar so you follow up with a phone call. Many people want to avoid this step but you must pick up the phone! I suggest calling two days after the letter should have been received, so if the letter would be received on a Tuesday, follow up on a Thursday.

Let's make it real – here's a process that will help

Be prepared – create a script and practise. You will find you sound clearer and less nervous if you stand up.

Never ask 'Is now a good time to call?' It never will be. Here's something you can adapt:

Hi, I'm (insert full name). My name may be familiar as I've recently contacted you.

My main strengths are in (add some detail – your overall summary).

I'm interested in (name of company) because – (and add some detail on why you got in touch).

Believe that you will be successful, don't let thoughts of failure get in the way

Start with calls to people you think will be easier, keep the more difficult ones till you have 'warmed up'.

The phone will probably be answered by the recipient's assistant, so develop rapport so that they want to help you. If asked the purpose of your call, say you have written to xxxx and are following up with a personal call. If they are unavailable, find out when would be a good time to ring.

They may try to put you off, not know anything about your letter, suggest you contact HR – or they may have been primed by their boss and be expecting your call. Let's hope it's this last one, and it could be if your letter is powerful enough!

If you get through to voicemail, make your message short – again you can have a script to read:

Hi, this is (your name) and I'm calling to follow up on my recent letter. I'll be available for the rest of the day on (insert your phone number and state it slowly). I'm looking forward to talking with you.

If they ask you to send in your CV ask them for the specific job title that you should refer to. You could say something like, *'Assuming my CV meets your needs, shall we pencil in a date to meet next week? I'm free on Tuesday and Wednesday, which is best for you?'*

Meetings

The purpose of writing and phone calls is to get a meeting. This is not a conventional interview, which may come later, but a chance to discuss the problems faced by the person you are talking with and how you can help. Initially these will be short conversations.

You've arranged to meet, so don't blow it. Make sure you plan effectively. Think about it from their point of view: you've raised their curiosity and there might be a possibility of an opening but they are likely to play it cool and to start off by telling you that there aren't any vacancies. Have questions planned but also be ready to answer any questions they may have. More details to help in Chapter 14, Interviews at 50+.

As preparation, consider doing research on their competitors – competitor analysis – and sharing this in the interview.

Afterwards send a thank-you note

Too many people focus on saying thanks for spending time with me. The real purpose of a thank-you note is **to address the issues you discussed at the meeting**. You went there to sell yourself, you asked searching questions, now follow up by demonstrating clear thought as to what was discussed.

- If you were talking about your copy-writing skills, provide some examples.
- If they told you about a problem, make a suggestion for how you can solve it.

You can send it by email but also follow up with a handwritten note. People read letters. Keep it short. Keep it simple, and make every word count. You can't prepare this in advance; you have to focus on what was discussed.

Send more of the initial letters

You will not get to meet with everyone you wrote to, so send out a second letter about three weeks later. Circumstances may have changed and they may now have a possible need for you. This time your letter should start in a different way; think about what you can say that would encourage the reader to continue reading. No need to refer to your last letter – write as if it is the first time.

You may not hear anything. Leave it a couple of weeks and then send a variation on the letter.

Next steps

If things were positive you should hear back to take things forward. This could be to come in for a formal interview so read Chapter 14, Interviews at 50+.

Case Study

Debra said: 'When my husband was unexpectedly made redundant last year he knew it would take him six months to move toward employment . . . even with an extensive professional network. It was LinkedIn, his own extensive network plus using networking events that proved invaluable. The job he now has was never advertised . . . the hidden job market and accessing it is a skill in itself.'

An alternative approach – knock on doors

For some people this approach will work. It's particularly useful for retail and for hands-on technical jobs such as mechanics. It worked well for Simon, who approached car showrooms.

Here's the approach.

Take your CV and go into every place of work, such as shops, or go to an industrial park and visit every organisation. For an office job don't start by handing your CV to the receptionist, visit first and tell them you are doing market research and ask for the name of the XXXX – whoever would be the person you would work for. You can then go back the next day with a personalised letter. Make sure the letter is clearly written.

How to do this for a retail position.

Go into the store, dressed smartly, and have a quick look around so you can make a meaningful comment and ask to speak to the manager. Physically hand over your CV. Do this in the early part of the day when it is quiet. Avoid trying to make contact if they are busy with customers.

Tell them how interested you are in the store/industry. Refer to what you already know about the company and/or what you have noticed as you look around. It can take several days to go round an industrial estate or shopping centre in your travel-to-work radius, such as Liverpool ONE or Bristol's Cabot Circus.

Case Study

This worked for Jemma who was living in central London and struggling to get work. She followed this approach around the posh clothes shops in W1 and in the fifth shop they asked her to work for a day, like an extended interview. This led to a job offer.

It's about getting work, it doesn't have to be a full-time job

This book is based around finding work, not necessarily a full-time permanent job. This can include offering to take on a project. This gets around the worry employers will have, especially small companies. They need to be sure that you will fit in and add value. It's similar to the 'temp to perm' type of work that recruitment agencies recruit for. More on this in Chapter 13, Alternatives to a permanent full-time job.

IN A NUTSHELL

You now know how to make a direct approach, and along with Chapter 7, Connecting with others, you have all you need to follow this effective approach to job-searching. I want you to significantly reduce the amount of time you spend on traditional approaches and make contacting organisations direct your priority.

This chapter has made clear how to do it, so follow the advice and enjoy. My clients have found it helpful and could see that getting a job in a competitive market is just like selling a product.

BEFORE YOU MOVE ON

- Make a note of three key points you have learnt.
- Make a note of what is the top takeaway, for you, from this chapter.

- **Have you created a plan to make your first direct approach?**

12 TRADITIONAL JOB SEARCH

A traditional job search, applying for advertised jobs, is a popular approach to finding a job, but is also one of the least effective.

If you are going to apply, you need to follow an effective approach. In this chapter you will:

■ learn how to choose relevant job sites

■ learn how to get the best out of recruiters

■ move beyond creating a LinkedIn profile to finding jobs via LinkedIn

■ learn how to find jobs through Google.

A pplying for jobs is not where you should focus your time; you are more likely to have success with the direct approach – see Chapter 10.

Applying for jobs works best for younger people seeking a similar job to what they have done before. As I write this chapter, two of my clients in their thirties got job offers following an application within just a few weeks of being made redundant. It's much more difficult for those of us at 50+; even if we get through shortlisting we can fail at interview, so **keep the traditional job search to about 20% of your time available** and make sure to make a stellar application.

Finding job vacancies

Job sites

There are masses of job sites. The main ones like Fish4jobs, Monster and Total Jobs might not necessarily be the best for you, so review different sites, look at the jobs advertised and decide if you are likely to find jobs there. In some cases smaller sites will be more relevant, those that focus on a particular niche. It can cost a lot of money to advertise on the major sites, so it is much more cost-effective for organisations to choose a more targeted means of advertising and they are more likely to get relevant applicants. If you want a job in the charity sector, then sites such as Charity People and Charity Job will be more relevant, etc.

Job sites allow you to search by a number of categories, e.g. location, field of work, salary, key word. Many job sites contain over 10,000 vacancies, and are updated every 24 hours, so you need to check sites regularly and learn how to use the relevant search criteria. Each site has its own quirks, so make a note so you get quicker results next time.

Recruiters and employers pay to 'view' CVs on these databases. The sites are designed to attract fees for looking at CVs. Some vacancies are fictitious, placed to 'harvest' CVs for recruiters' own databases. The sites want your CV so they can sell your details to recruiters. On one site the fee is £170+VAT for one day's access and the chance to download 50 CVs, and £225+VAT for seven days' access and to download up to 100 CVs a day.

Job aggregators

It might be more useful to use a job aggregator, a site which brings together job ads from a number of different job sites, newspaper job sections, company career pages, recruitment agencies and more, and which will save you a great deal of time. Choose sites such as Indeed.com available in 50 countries and 28 languages and Simplyhired.co.uk, available in 24 countries and 12 languages. You must set clear parameters so you aren't swamped with job suggestions. Of course you may end up with duplicate postings but these are easy to spot and you are unlikely to apply more than once.

Indeed works by trawling through job postings found online and brings them together like Google. You can also upload your CV directly to the site.

Simplyhired has integrated Facebook into its search engine so it means that you can search for jobs at friends' companies, an interesting combination of job-searching and social networking. With Social-hire you can set up an online profile using your LinkedIn, Twitter or Facebook account or create a standalone account to ensure anonymity.

Careerjet.co.uk is an employment search engine that I only found when researching for this book. At the time of writing, their website says: 'In just one search access 40,657,384 jobs published on 28,560 websites in the world.' You may also like to consider vacancycentral.co.uk.

Don't forget **jackalopejobs.com** which also allows you to find people you know who work for the companies you want to apply to, found via your social-media connections.

Case Study

Gary had a very poor technique: he hadn't set up alerts, focused on using just two sites (he didn't know of job aggregator sites) and made at least 20 applications a week, but none targeted a specific job. Gary felt that he was making good progress as he was counting the number of applications. Once I got him to focus on a goal of getting shortlisted for interview, he realised that the best way forward was to make fewer applications that were very well done.

Register on job sites
You need to evaluate a site before you upload your details, so be cautious if you have to register first. Always read (and print) the privacy policy. I know

it is a faff but you will see if they are likely to sell or rent your email address. You can also see the access they give to recruiters. How much do they charge to access your information? Monitor for changes on a regular basis.

Make sure you can delete your CV once you get a new job – you don't want your new employer to think you are already looking for a new job.

Be mindful of identity theft. Before you upload your details make sure you can conceal your identity and protect your contact information. Check what personal information you can block. If you are currently in employment, you may want to block your CV being found by recruiters – you will find the jobs to apply for. You may also prefer to block your address or phone number. Yes, it can make us more difficult to contact, but demonstrates we are savvy web users.

Beware, some sites have been set up to harvest CVs and personal information. These are fake job sites that look real with a privacy policy, terms of use and 'Contact us' page. Before uploading your CV and personal details check out the phone number and see if it is answered.

As you review sites, check that you can quickly find the job you want based on your criteria. If you find it awkward, ignore the site, there are plenty of others. Also make sure they have the jobs you seek – there is little point looking for jobs in engineering in the North West on a site that covers catering opportunities in the South East.

Some sites have lots of jobs listed but these vacancies may have been filled yet left up to give the impression of a lot of vacancies. Be wary of sites that don't show a date of posting.

Some sites allow you to upload more than one version of your CV, which is helpful if you have a few jobs that you are interested in. Keep track of which versions of your CV are where and also the parameters you have set.

Ideally the jobs will be posted by an employer but many will be via agencies. They won't provide the name of the organisation as you could then go to them direct and they won't get their fee.

Set up a separate email account just for job applications, as you may find your email address compromised and used to send spam messages to you. Also, once you have a new job you can close this account.

Richard found this advice very helpful, and said he had been surprised by the amount of spam signing up on websites can lead to.

When you register on these websites, job details will be sent direct to your inbox. Be too vague in your requirements and you will be inundated, so focus on your targeted job area. Some of the emails will try to persuade you to sign up for courses that are not worth the money, or to get you interested in commission-only jobs or starting a franchise, so be careful.

To create a cyber-safe CV, you can modify your employment history. Remove your current employer's name; replace it with an *accurate, but generic* description so 'XYZ engineering company' becomes 'engineering company' and if you work for NEXT it is 'a large retail chain'. You can adapt your job title, too, if it is very specific to your industry. Most of the people I've worked with liked this idea – 'Very helpful,' said Anita.

Key tips

- Register and store your user ID and password.
- Review the privacy policy before adding any personal data – never post your actual birth date or NI number online, nor show your full home address.
- Set up a free email account so it's easy to close it down once you get a new job.
- Upload your CV and make a note of which version is uploaded. If you can, copy and paste text in so you can make changes.
- Save as you go in case of power surges.
- Don't include your year of birth, it could be used against you.
- You may find some optional questions which are probably competency-based; take time to review and consider. Don't just answer off the top of your head.
- The 'additional information' section is a good place to include your cover letter content.

Working with recruiters

Will you find your next job through a recruitment consultant? Probably not, the staff tend to be young and most don't have a good reputation for working with older job-seekers. It <u>may</u> work if you want to get a job similar to the one you did before, but there's not a high level of probability.

Recruitment agencies earn fees if a CV they submit in response to a vacancy is accepted and the applicant is employed. The fee is a percentage of the first year's salary, often 15–25%. A lot of companies are regarding recruiters as a bit of an expensive luxury so they use LinkedIn and seek referrals.

Valerie's first thought was to register with agencies. That's where you get local jobs, she said to me. But recruiters, in general, tend to perceive older workers as being hard to place. They see us as too expensive, that we won't fit in with the 'dynamic' culture and are less productive. We stand a better chance with smaller niche agencies. These are often set up by older recruiters and seem to have a better understanding of and commitment to people of our age.

If a recruiter gets in touch it is often to set up a first meeting, so the interview chapter is relevant. If you have 'de-aged' your CV they may be expecting someone under 40 so you need to help manage this initial shock. You have to appear youthful (both what you wear and how you move) and come across as likeable.

Valerie met with three recruiters and said that they all seemed below 30. None put her forward for the jobs she was interested in and she had a strong suspicion it was due to her age.

Recruiters make immediate judgements; they assume their clients don't want someone older. They are generally paid on results and don't want to put someone forward who may be unlikely to get the job. **This is why we will struggle**.

We need to understand our strengths but also appreciate that getting a job through a recruiter is unlikely; we need to make a direct approach.

Local vacancies

Many smaller organisations will often use the local press to advertise, so it's worth checking in the local paper.

LinkedIn

You should now have an effective profile, but you also need to use the site well. Follow companies to find details of job ads and also use the search for jobs to find out what to apply for. Other jobs may also be found within the groups that you belong to. You also want recruiters to find you on LinkedIn.

Recruiters use key words to search LinkedIn profiles. Results show up based on the degree of separation and presence of the search term.

This is why it helps to become first-*degree* connected to as many recruiters as possible. They are the ones making the most searches. Having recruiters in your network increases your chances of being found.

Your profile should describe you as accurately as possible using words the recruiter will search for.

Are you being found?

Use the 'Who's Viewed Your Profile' section on the right side of your home page; you can also get there directly by clicking: www.linkedin.com/wvmx/profile.

On this page you'll find the 'Trends' box with a graph in it called 'Views'. If you are not seeing an upward trend, make changes to your photo, headline and increase the number of recommendations. These have the greatest impact on click rates. By making small changes to these three elements, you will begin to see increases in the number of times your profile was viewed.

Other places to find job vacancies

Company websites – Many organisations have a career page with details of current vacancies; they don't always put details on external sites. They have a view that if you want to work for their company you should be looking on their site.

Using Google to get a job – If you want to be a marketing executive in Bristol, for example, you go to http://google.co.uk and enter *(~jobs OR ~careers)* 'marketing executive' Bristol and you will find specific jobs from a range of agencies. The first part of this search tells Google that you are seeking web pages that contain words related to either 'jobs' or 'careers'. By putting these words in brackets it makes it clear to Google that you want pages with either of these words.

The second part tells Google the job that you seek. By putting this in quotes it means that you want these two words to appear together separated by a space. The final part shows the location.

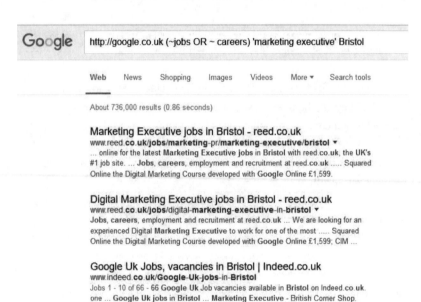

Once you have found some really great searches, you can save them as an 'alert' and have new pages sent to you as they occur. You can set an alert at www.google.co.uk/alerts. Most of the people I work with didn't really understand how this could help before, but all found it a helpful tip, and you should too.

Professional associations – These will often have a job-search service. Companies that want to recruit members of a professional body may recruit that way.

Other publications – Don't forget to consider jobs you see advertised on gumtree.com/jobs, and craigslist. You can also use the advanced search option on Google and choose e.g. 'job board' + 'retail' and on Twitter – twitjobsearch, e.g. 'project manager in London'. Of course you can also search on Google, e.g. 'Bristol management accountant jobs'.

Help wanted ads – For some it is worth looking at old-style methods. You may see a 'help wanted' advert in the window or outside a place of work. Just yesterday I saw a sign saying 'Recruiting Technicians Now' as I drove into Cheltenham. Simon eventually got a job through seeing a job ad outside a new car dealership and now collects and delivers high-end cars to customers.

Look internally – And if you are currently employed, don't forget about looking internally to see what opportunities there are. It's not just about seeing jobs that are advertised, you can also build relationships with people so you get to hear of internal opportunities, perhaps to start on a project that becomes a full-time job.

The process
Avoid getting distracted by applying for jobs you are not qualified for.

1. Daily approach – identify jobs to apply for
Don't be seduced into spending many hours a day on job sites and think you are following effective job-search techniques. Limit your time and be highly focused. The more you set up alerts, the easier it will be.

Each day review new job postings and choose what to apply for
You will not make five to ten applications a day, and it's unlikely to be that many in a week unless you are very clear on what you want, such as Anita applying for legal executive jobs. She was able to send the same CV and

supporting information to almost every job ad. Most people need to tailor their application and this will take time.

If your preparation is good you will mainly receive job details on jobs where there is a close match. Ignore any others that have slipped through. Your time is valuable, don't be distracted.

You may get excited as there are lots of jobs that meet your criteria, but beware. Not all advertised jobs exist. Some agencies trawl for CVs and there is no specific job, so don't build your hopes up.

Not all job ads are current, some ads are left up despite already being filled. This really miffs the people I work with who waste time applying for a job they can never be shortlisted for. The job ad remains as the recruiter has paid for e.g. 30 days and wants to leave the ad up for publicity. There may be another job coming up soon, so it helps the recruiter, especially an agency, to build a pool of people that could fill the job in the future.

Many agencies/recruiters are paid on contingency terms – they only get paid after a placement is made, so they want to be able to fill a vacancy fast. A recruiter may anticipate a job needing to be filled and post an ad to allow them to respond fast to one of their clients (client companies love this type of fast response). Recruiters seeking to fill temporary posts need to be able to provide shortlisted candidates within 12 hours so they need a good number of people they can call on.

Companies may also place ads for non-existent jobs to provide the illusion to their competitors that they are doing well, and also to see who from their competitors applies, thus spotting competitor vulnerability.

It may still be worth a review of your local/regional newspaper and professional journal, so make a note which days the ads will appear.

Searching on job sites takes up time but is not efficient job-hunting. You shouldn't spend more than about 20% of your available time identifying jobs to apply for; you need to spend much more time on research and meeting people.

On job-search boards make minor changes at least a couple of times a week to keep your details near the top of a searcher's list. Your CVs are shown in the order they have been uploaded/revised. The more recent, the better.

2. Take a detailed review of the job ad(s)
Print out the job posts and highlight the key requirements. Compare your skills and experience and confirm you are a close match.

Carefully read the job description, duties and responsibilities. Alongside targeting your application you also want to make sure that you meet the criteria and confirm this is a job you would want to do.

Employers want people who completely match with the job spec. So carefully analyse the ad and make sure you can provide examples of everything they seek. Also review all the achievement bullets on your CV to make sure you have included the best examples for this particular vacancy.

Check if there is a specific requirement such as to provide a specific example, and make sure you include it. People like Gary who fire off applications to everything they see are likely to miss this.

Go beyond the job ad and consider what else may enhance your application. You may have skills which may not be specified in the advert but could be of interest to the prospective employer.

In a buoyant market you could apply for jobs where you don't fully match, but when there are many applicants, employers can be very choosy. Before you dive into an in-depth and comprehensive application, make sure you can provide specific examples of how you meet the job requirements.

They are asking for a degree! Often a degree is a mandatory requirement. Back in 1973 when I was 16, few stayed on for A levels. Over half of my year left and got a job. In my twenties I went on to study for a degree with the Open University. I'd put 'degree calibre' on your CV if the job demands one and you don't have one.

The closing date may change, so don't be caught out. A job post may be taken down early if the hiring manager decides they already have enough applications. Be ready to apply by having standard passages you can cut and paste into a job application and then customise to a particular job.

A simple way to confirm you match the job spec is to print out the job ad and use a highlighter pen to highlight the key requirements. You can then create two columns. Put the requirements from the ad on the left and your examples on the right. For example, if the ad says 'self-starter', refer to examples of where you have taken the initiative.

You can use this research to adapt your CV for a particular job and to write the cover letter/supporting statement. This analysis will show you where you are strong and where you lack expertise.

Their needs	My experience/skills
Over five years' experience of working in a customer-focused environment	Nearly five years in prestigious serviced office environment, three-and-a-half of which were spent in a managerial role in charge of front-of-house and customer-service teams
Proven successful track record of training and motivating staff	Reduced staff turnover and increased number of internal promotions by building empowered, goal-driven teams; created and implemented staff training and development programme; maintained high staff morale and a co-operative working environment; coached and mentored underperformers; rewarded exceptional performance
Proven HR experience to carry out appraisals and disciplinary procedures	Conducted regular performance reviews and annual appraisals; obtained 360-degree feedback; created and implemented individual and team performance plans; carried out disciplinary procedures
High customer focus	Achieved on average 95% customer satisfaction; increased client retention to over 90%; formally recognised for delivering excellent service

Use this approach to ensure you have the best examples in your CV. It can also form the basis of your cover letter.

> **Case Study**
>
> Richard said that he found this very helpful, as it was easy to see where you don't match and which ads to focus more time on.

3. Gather relevant information (research)

Some ads are very brief, so be proactive and phone the organisation to find out more about the job. It's not 100% certain you will get to speak with someone, but be positive and try to speak to the recruiter. Have your accomplishments ready in case you are asked questions.

The sorts of questions you should ask include the following.

- What is the exact job title?
- Who does the person report to?
- What specific experience are you looking for?
- What are the most important tasks that will need to be done?
- What factors would cause a candidate to be eliminated from consideration?
- Is this a new position? If not, what happened to the previous job-holder?
- What qualifications are essential?
- Are there specific problems you will want the new employee to solve?

If the relevant person is not available to speak to you, ask for the job description and person specification. These will help you to create your cover letter and adapt your CV, or help with completing an application form. You can then continue comparing your experience and skills with the requirements.

You may not always get more information, so use the research you undertook as you considered what jobs to apply for.

You have already demonstrated you match up through the two-column approach, now you can focus on your application. Review and revise your CV or complete an application, also write a cover letter or use the 'further information' section on an application form to explain your suitability for the job.

Depending on the job you seek you can go beyond a review of the website (which is all that most people do) and undertake some competitor analysis. You want to make sure that this is an organisation that you would want to work for.

If you are, for example, applying for a job somewhere that serves the public, visit one of their stores/outlets to do an undercover 'reccy'.

With all of this information you can create a SWOT analysis (Strengths, Weaknesses, Opportunities and Threats) or a PESTLE review (Political, Economic, Social, Technological, Legal and Environmental Issues). It took some time to convince Gary to understand why he needed to do this, but once he started proper research alongside getting focused on the type of job to apply for he got two interviews out of four applications so was convinced.

Specific websites will let you know more about what employees think. Look at **Glassdoor** which provides information on employees' views on a company, salary rankings and interview questions. Also consider **TheJobCrowd** which gives reviews by employees of their company including ratings for work-life balance, career progression, remuneration and interview tips, and **TARGETjobs** which includes details from company publicity alongside tips to get hired.

Don't forget to use printed reference materials. Your local business library will have copies of Kompass Business Directory for you to review. You can also access this material online at – http://gb.kompass.com/b/business-directory.

Use LMI
I discussed the importance of labour market information (LMI) in Chapter 3 for identifying areas of growth. Use LMI later to demonstrate to a potential employer that you understand the sector or industry. Make it clear you understand the challenges they face and how well you match up.

4. Review your CV
Review your master CV to see if you can enhance any of the achievement bullets to be more focused on the specific job requirements. If the job description requires someone with great organisational skills, highlight on your CV a job or project in which you demonstrated your strengths in organisation. If

it stresses the need for leadership qualities, you must include an example of a time when you displayed leadership skills.

Read through your CV with fresh eyes and make sure that as many of the examples as possible relate to this particular job. You may want to re-order some of your bullets.

Consider the size of the organisation and again adapt your examples. If applying to a large organisation, highlight your experience working for large organisations; for a small organisation, show how you can transfer your skills to a niche player, how you can work in a small team and how you are happy to muck in when there is pressure on time.

Case Study

Gary's CV lacked focus as he was chasing too many options. Once he made the decision to target hardware test engineer jobs it really focused his job search.

When submitting an application via an online portal, shortlisting will be done through your use of key words, but once you get through this stage, your letter will be reviewed. Other organisations still review each application on an individual basis. Help the recruiter by showing them how you match up.

Cover letters and e-notes

The cover letter was always considered an essential part of an application, but that was before automatic software was used for shortlisting. It will have more impact when you are sending your CV to an individual, such as when applying to a smaller company where a real person does the shortlisting. But, when you get through the software shortlisting your CV, this and your cover letter will be read by a human, so it is still needed.

Too many cover letters are boring

They start with the dreary *'I'm writing to apply ...'* and go on and on, far too long and thus lose the reader's attention. You may have read that you need to address every point in the job ad; that might have worked in the past, but no longer. Aim for just one page, and leave some white space around your words.

> **Case Study**
> Gary's cover letter started off with saying that he had been made
> redundant. I got him to change his approach; this wasn't explaining why he
> should get the job. We started to include key information from his research,
> and along with a revised CV, he started to get shortlisted.

The process for creating a great cover letter

You have reviewed the ad and highlighted all key terms and words. If you get
additional information such as a job and person spec you will have further
information to review. You should have done this already, as you were getting
ready to make an application. Now review your preparation to create the cover
letter.

Pick out what is key

Occasionally you may find as many as 20-plus key criteria, far too many for
you to address using the approach I'm going to share, so you have to stick with
what is key – just four or five points. Usually these are the ones that will have
been included in the job ad.

It can be tempting to want to address every one of the criteria, but imagine
how you would feel faced with a four-page cover letter; you must focus
on what is key. Include too much and your application is heading for
the bin.

If there's an option to also post your CV, being 'retro' can help you to stand out.
You can include a printed cover letter, created to match your CV, in a 'house
style' with the same font.

In general, those who are 50+ really excel in the written word compared to
many younger job-seekers who seem to have difficulty writing clearly and using
grammar correctly.

Opening up a separate document can be seen as a chore so it might be
preferable to include the content in the body of the email (an e-note).
This makes it easier for the reader to view, one less document to click, but

this means you have less opportunity to format and layout to your choice, particularly if you use a plain text email.

Long boring cover letters are out, you must focus on what is key and keep the letter to one side with a decent amount of white space in the margins.

Letter / e-note style
Here is a structure to follow.

Name of the person you are writing to – You must make it personal and include the person's name, even if it wasn't included in the job ad. Demonstrate some initiative by tracking down the name of the person you should write to. Research on Google or LinkedIn, or call the organisation.

Opening paragraph – Have a strong opening sentence focused on your strengths for this job. Make it exciting, and personal. You want them to know that this letter is being sent just to them and not to a hundred other companies. Make it clear why you are writing, but avoid typing *'I am writing …'*

Middle paragraph(s) – It's better to include two shorter paragraphs than one dense block of text. Your goal here is to show how you can be useful to this particular organisation – make it clear why they should shortlist you.

Describe what strengths you have to offer this employer by showing the relationship between your skills and experience and the requirements of the vacant role. You can also describe your previous achievements and how they relate to the role, and identify three reasons why you should be called for interview. Be quantifiable where you can – what results can the company expect to get if they recruit you?

A popular approach to this middle section lays out information in two columns: on the left you include their requirements and on the right how you match up. Earlier on you saw an example of evidence laid out in two columns; this can be used to style your cover letter.

Their needs	My experience/skills

However, you don't need to present in two columns. You can use 'Their needs' as a heading, in bold, and the follow with your example of experience or skills, such as:

High customer focus – *Achieved on average 95% customer satisfaction; increased client retention to over 90%; formally recognised for delivering excellent service.*

This makes it very easy for a recruiter to see that you have given some thought to how you match up and can be useful but not if it takes up too many words and detracts from the message you want to give. You still need to keep it to one page.

Closing paragraph – Reiterate your enthusiasm for the job and say what you will do next, i.e. wait to hear from them or phone the next week.

You could include the cover letter along with your CV as a three-page PDF.

The new-style cover letter

A CV gets a nine-second skim. How long do you think is spent on the cover letter? That's why many people are now producing a *very* short letter, less than 150 words. When you use this type of cover letter you make every word count.

For the email think beyond the job title. Think of at least four alternative subject headers, and think from the reader's perspective: which will make them want to read on? How can you build on the job title? Gary used 'Your next test engineer'.

In your first short paragraph provide a match between your position, industry, specialisation, and value-added qualifications and the job you're applying for.

In your second short paragraph or list of three bullet points list the benefits you have delivered that match what the recruiter will be looking for from a new recruit – use numbers such as currency and percentages. Every word must count so use key words to show how you match up. You've got to quickly get them interested and to make them care about you

In your last paragraph state that you would like to meet in person to discuss the value you can bring to the organisation.

You can also take note of marketing professionals and end with a PS – *'Call me today to learn about how I can help you to increase customer satisfaction/ increase profit/something else'* – that would make them want to talk with you.

> ## Case Study
>
> Sue applied for 60+ jobs via jobsites and never got shortlisted despite considering herself a strong fit. She finally found a job via someone she knew, only making a formal application after getting the job offer, and just doing this to satisfy HR.

Application forms

Some organisations, especially in the public sector, prefer application forms. These make it quick and easy to compare applications from a number of different people as the information is presented in a standard way.

Application forms vary in length and will include factual information about you and about your education, career, health and interests. They will usually include open-ended questions about your reasons for applying for the job and the contribution that you think you can make.

The first application form can be very time-consuming, so save all the detail in a Word document and you should be able to edit and use it again in future applications.

The basics

Read the instructions carefully before you start. Make sure you understand what information is needed and where. Always keep in mind the particular requirements of the job for which you are applying. That is why the initial analysis is so helpful.

Some application forms are Word documents you can save offline, complete and then email, but many are completed online. You can still type offline to ensure your responses are grammatically correct, without typos, and then copy and paste in the details later.

With an online form, the text boxes for you to type in may be fixed (and you may have a set number of words or characters to use) or they may expand to include unlimited information. If you are given, for example, 100 words for your reply, aim to be as close as possible to the word limit.

Some questions will require brief, factual answers. Others will seek a narrative answer; this should be drafted and redrafted so that it is as good as it can be. **You still need to personalise your application to the job ad.**

Additional information (also known as the personal statement)

Usually there is a section for you to provide further information in support of your application; it's similar to what you would include in a cover letter but you generally have more space available. This is often the section that interviewers read most carefully. Make sure you include information on why you want the job and what makes you the right candidate. Wherever you can, bring out your strengths, skills and achievements; don't focus on your job responsibilities.

Strengthen your application by stating a key reason for being considered for the job and backing it up immediately with an example. If possible, use terms from the advertisement for your main reasons; continue for two or three key points, substantiating each general statement with an example. This can make your application very persuasive and penetrating.

Imagine you are asked at interview 'Why should we appoint you?' Your answer to that question could be all the things to be brought out in the open-ended section.

This is also the place to demonstrate the research you have undertaken. Few people research properly, so show you have found out about the organisation, the industry and how you can solve some of their challenges.

Competency-based questions

Some application forms will ask you to provide details about your experience in some specific areas against a number of headings. These are likely to be the competences you are assessed on throughout the selection process, so you must provide very clear examples. Such forms may appear complicated but are a structured approach to selling yourself through the application process. Once you understand the structure you can also use this with interview preparation.

The best approach to take is to use CAR – First describe the **Challenge**, follow up with the **Action** you took – what you did and why, and then the **Result**. Summarise the results of your actions.

The competences included will have been identified by the employer through the job-analysis process, and will be key skills or personal qualities needed for the job. The questions generally include some guidance, such as:

For each scenario you are asked to describe a situation (ideally fairly recent) from your own experience, which you think is the best example of what you have done and which demonstrates the specified ability.

Your answer can draw on your experiences in any kind of setting, not just paid employment, so include any good examples from your hobby or volunteering. Here's an example.

Describe a time when your ethics were challenged and how you responded. *'I was working at a plant for a major auto manufacturer and I had a colleague visiting the plant for internal audit purposes. When this auditor asked my manager whether or not certain forms had been signed to authorise the use of company vehicles, he lied to the auditor, saying that the forms had been signed when they really hadn't been. And I knew this. My dilemma was whether I should tell the auditor that my manager had lied or just keep quiet. Ultimately, I decided to tell the auditor privately that we didn't have a process in place for authorising vehicles' usage. I told the auditor that my manager probably misunderstood the question even though I knew full-well that he hadn't. In this way, I let the auditor know we were not in compliance, but at the same time I chose to do it in a way that maintained my relationship with my manager. At the time, I felt that it was the best decision I could make – one that was in the best interest of my company which also didn't break the trust I had with my manager.'*

I've provided more guidance to competency-based questions in Chapter 14, Interviews at 50+.

Unusual questions

Some companies ask questions that are a bit out of the ordinary. For example, apply for a job with Innocent and you will be asked to respond to a number of questions including these, with my suggestions on how to answer.

- *You'd never know it but I can …* You need to write something quirky to make you stand out.

- *We love meeting people who leave things a bit better than they find them. So please tell us about a recent situation where you took the initiative and made something happen …* This is a place to provide a competency-based reply.
- *We're looking for people who face challenges head on and deliver against the odds. What achievement are you most proud of?* Think of a specific example and be sure to include *why*.

Questions are often included to see how you think and to see if you are willing to step outside the answers most provide. The best way to answer questions is to make good use of your background but make it relevant to the organisation. In the case of applying for a job, look through the company website and find out as much as you can about their culture and style so examples can be chosen that are likely to suit the organisational norms.

Submitting an application form
Remember, if the form asks you not to send a CV with it, don't. Check that your answers on the application form mirror information on your CV and LinkedIn profile. When you have completed the application form, check it very carefully then hit the 'submit' button.

Submit applications and follow up
Within just a few hours of a job post being listed many people will apply, that's why an earlier application can be better as sometimes recruiters say 'enough is enough' and don't look at any more.

Professional Advice
Did you know that 30% of job applications are submitted within the first three days a job is posted? Or that if you apply to a job within the first three days, you are 13% more likely to land the role?

Daniel Ayele, LinkedIn Official Blog
(blog.linkedin.com/2015/01/29/jobseeking-tips)

Don't forget that whether you upload your CV to a database or apply for a specific vacancy, in most cases your CV will be 'read' by software for relevancy. Read again the CV section, Chapter 8, which explains about ATS. You may like to have a plain text version of your CV with less formatting, and omitting any images, graphs and charts so these don't get corrupted through the software parsing.

Submitting CVs and applications via email

When submitting a CV or job application by email, treat it just like a written approach with a proper letter/e-note, not just a short email saying 'Here is my CV'. Include details such as job title, reference number, name, etc. When attaching your CV, do not name the file 'CV' – how will the recruiter find this again? It is much better to name it, for example, 'DtaylorCV' or even better 'DTaylor_Projectmgt_expert'.

Who do you know?

If you know someone who works for the company you want to work for, they could deliver your CV direct to the desk of the person doing the shortlisting, with a personal recommendation. Your CV will get much more than the usual cursory glance. (This is unlikely to work in a public sector organisation as they usually have a 'no canvassing' rule.)

You may not realise you know someone, so check though the people you are connected with on LinkedIn.

Case Study

Richard said: 'I cannot emphasise enough how helpful this was to me getting my new job. It was through people I know making the introduction that led to interviews, they were my advocates. At two of my interviews, my advocates understood my background and could explain why I'd be perfect for the job in a way no type of CV could have done.'

Post a hard copy

You can send a hard copy of your CV to the recruiter, and if you have the information, you can also send it to the person who would be your manager. This is an opportunity to post your CV on nice paper, and to create a more visually appealing design than the plain text one you may have uploaded to an ATS program.

Follow up

If a couple of weeks have gone by and you haven't heard anything, you can send a friendly follow-up email, and use this opportunity to remind them of one of your strengths.

IN A NUTSHELL

We've made good progress in this book, making sure you are focused on finding job ads and making effective applications. This has included application forms, cover letters and e-notes and why sending a hard-copy CV is helpful. I've made it clear this isn't the best way to get your next job; you need to take more control, take a direct approach and target the hidden job market so re-read the previous chapter.

ACTIVITY 31

BEFORE YOU MOVE ON

- Make a note of three key points you have learnt.
- Make a note of what is the top takeaway, for you, from this chapter.

- **Critically review your approach to job applications.**

13 ALTERNATIVES TO A PERMANENT FULL-TIME JOB

Most of my clients come to me seeking a permanent full-time job. I encourage them, and you, to think more broadly when searching for work. This does not necessarily mean looking at poorly paid hourly activity; there are many different options and this chapter covers them.

We may need to find our own work, to become self-employed. This can be a fundamental shift in thinking for all, but especially for those of us who were led to believe in a job for life.

In this chapter you will learn more to enable you to consider:

■ taking a self-employment/consultancy route to work on projects

■ interim management

■ project working

■ portfolio working

■ freelance working

■ survival job options.

We will also discuss how much to charge and why it may sometimes be worthwhile to work for free.

The work we did in earlier chapters about understanding who we are and what we can offer is an important step to finding work. We need to be clear on the skills and experience we have, which others might pay for.

What can you offer?

In many cases this can be consultancy but there are plenty of other options to consider, some based on experience gained through a hobby such as cake decoration.

Most options will need us to be technically savvy – we need to be able to run our website, or pay someone to do this for us. Excellent communication skills are also required.

ACTIVITY 32

DO YOU HAVE THE PERSONAL QUALITIES TO SUCCEED?

Alongside our skills and experience we also need certain personal qualities. Be honest with yourself: can you say yes to these?

- Strong work ethic
- Adaptable
- Organised
- Self-motivated with a can-do attitude
- Assertive
- Focused
- Independent
- Take the initiative
- Multitasking

If not, what can you do to help develop skill in these areas? Chapter 16 will help.

Interim management/contracting

Interims are experienced managers and directors who are taken on to cover a functional role or to manage a short-term project. It's one area where age is a definite advantage and many senior staff see this as their first choice following redundancy. To do similar work but for a different organisation, and to draw in two or three times the amount previously earned.

But many times it doesn't work out. The first task is to get your first assignment and it's hard. You need to utilise people you know or quickly build up new relationships so re-reading Chapter 7 will help.

Definitely contact your previous employers, and if you have recently been made redundant you may be able to continue to work with your last employer. Ray is doing this for three days a week, which pays him the same each month as he previously earned as a full-time employee.

As a former employee you know the company culture and you have a track record, plus you know the staff, and your former colleagues are more likely to trust you.

Contact your previous manager and colleagues. Don't directly ask if they have any work but ask how they are getting on, listen for any problems and then you can suggest how you could help. This could lead to a project as a first piece of work.

Consider also contracting – approach a company with a bio that makes clear your skills, and how you can apply them to a project.

Professional Advice

A career in interim management is today a very real opportunity for many. Office of National Statistics figures on the self-employed in the UK have shown that many more people entering self-employment are choosing to stay self-employed, rather than it simply being a bridge to their next permanent job.

The interim management market has almost doubled in size (Ipsos-Mori Interim Management Association (IMA) Survey) since 2006 and today is estimated at circa £1.5bn and is a thriving market where interim managers support organisations at every level, from executive level assignments on the boards of companies, to project management of business and technical projects.

There are a number of factors that we would recommend for anyone considering an interim management career.

– Think of yourself as a business from day one, not just looking for a job.
– Understand your 'value proposition' quickly and keep it consistent, i.e. what is it that you are a specialist in and can demonstrably deliver for an organisation?
– Seek out professional interim service providers, like those within the IMA (http://www.interimmanagement.uk.com/).
– Make sure you continue to build and develop your personal and online network. The key to success is 'being found' by interim service providers and prospective clients.
– Remember, every assignment needs to be a reference for your next assignment . . . so deliver value for money every day you are working.

Simon Drake, Director of Executive Recruitment,
Search and Interim, Penna Plc

Project working/act like a consultant

Many organisations are hesitant about appointing permanent staff – will you fit in, is there enough work? They are far more amenable to taking on people for short-term projects.

This is similar to contracting but instead of e.g. a six-month contract, you work on a short-term assignment for a few weeks. This can demonstrate what you can do and allow you to build from one project to another.

Why not approach a prospective employer with a short proposal (can you do it in 200 words?) of what you could do to help their company.

■ Be very clear on your strengths and what you have to offer.
■ Research the sorts of companies that could use your help.
■ Think about something you could do, e.g. a project taking a couple of weeks or a month.
■ Write a short letter explaining how you can help with a particular situation. You could include how they only need to pay if they see results.
■ Include an informal proposal and perhaps an example of your work.
■ If you are looking for a job as a trainer, you could prepare and send a sample course that the company doesn't currently offer. If you are a sales

person you could research the competition and make suggestions. This could turn into a competitor analysis with graphs and charts, and you could send this to the managing director.

- Follow up with a phone call and arrange to meet.
- Chances are you will get paid!

You could seek out e.g. three companies all ready to employ you for a day a week each.

Act like a consultant

Do you have a shortlist of dream companies? Set up news alerts to see what comes up and follow them on LinkedIn, Twitter and Facebook. You have to follow them very carefully; you are looking to identify any problems they may have or challenges to overcome. As a consultant, you need to ascertain what sort of help you could provide. How can you be seen as an expert rather than as a job-hunter?

Now you need to show what you know about them. Think about their needs. Create a one-page job proposal to demonstrate your unique experiences, knowledge and ideas and which shows that you can make the organisation successful. **Only include how you can help, not what you would do** – sell the sizzle not the steak.

Approach a particular person within the company to discuss this draft proposal. If you get their agreement, you could get paid to carry out your proposal and this may lead on to a job offer, or at the very least provide an interesting addition to your CV.

Fees

How much to charge?

Working as a consultant you need to quote a fee that reflects that you aren't getting holiday benefits, sickness pay, or pension contribution and also the time needed to seek work in between projects. You should also expect to spend at least 20% of your time on marketing.

You also need to pay for your own training and development. This takes both time and money, and it's imperative that your skills are up to date, and ahead of the employees doing similar work.

Most people work for 240 days a year when you allow for holidays, so if your salary was £35,000 this works out at £146 per day. You would want to quote around double this figure. The fee will depend on what someone is willing to pay, and you may be prepared to quote a lower figure for a first project, but remember once you quote a fee with one organisation it may be hard to raise your fee.

Work for free?
Sometimes it is worth offering to work at no charge for one day a week for a month, or for payment only upon meeting the agreed objectives by the end of that month. This would provide a beneficial addition to your CV, and may even lead to a job offer. At the least it will get you a recommendation to help with getting further work.

Portfolio working
A portfolio career is a way of working where you have more than one job. This could include working two days developing your own catering business and three days working in your main career as an accountant. Or it could be to use your area of specialism and perhaps have a portfolio that includes consultancy, one-to-one advice work, training courses/seminars and writing. This is how I work.

People like us will often move into portfolio working following redundancy. The redundancy payment provides a financial cushion as we get started. The portfolio career is not necessarily highly paid consulting and contract work. People can choose to include some lower paid (or even unpaid) but personally rewarding work as part of their portfolio.

When people are considering a portfolio career this will generally be using the high-level skills gained from their profession such as PR director, or management accountant, but there are other skills required, such as being organised and feeling comfortable juggling a varied work load; see Activity 32.

Generally it will be self-driven people who will seek the right range of options to give them their own desired portfolio career. They usually need to be willing to network to meet people and to keep going in the face of knockbacks. There's also a need to be assertive and to be aware of boundaries, otherwise there is a danger that clients may pose too many demands and you find yourself working two three-day-a-week jobs, not two two-day jobs, and maybe only getting paid for two lots of two days.

A portfolio career can be a great way to gain experience in a new area, whilst maintaining three or four days a week doing a job in line with your experience and professional background.

The main cost is personal in managing time and maintaining a balance – sometimes it can be a difficult juggling act if your portfolio career consists of a few different things which may all involve deadlines at the same time.

If you are thinking about this, then weigh up what you want to do and how you will get this work. Think also if you can deal with the possible lack of security, although some may say that a portfolio career would give you greater career stability.

Freelance working

There are many things you could do on a freelance basis; of course it depends on your background. This list provides ideas of things to consider, such as producing something or providing a service. It is not an exhaustive list!

1. Bookkeeping
2. Build flat-pack furniture
3. Cater for a dinner party/lunches
4. Cleaning – be very special
5. Clutter clearing
6. Concierge service – collect cleaning, wait in for deliveries, etc.
7. Dog-walking
8. Freelance writing/editing/proofreading
9. Gardening services
10. Graphic designer
11. Grow and sell plants

12. Handyman/woman
13. Internet business – you can sell business services on fiverr.com
14. IT help desk – focus on home users?
15. Jewellery – create and sell on Etsy or eBay or at craft fairs
16. Making jam, cakes, etc.
17. Musician – gigs or teaching
18. Party organiser
19. Personal appliance testing
20. Personal trainer
21. Provide hospitality to language students
22. Public speaking – approach Probus, Women's Institute, etc., and offer to talk on an area of specialism; you should easily get £50 per hour
23. Rent out a spare room or offer B&B
24. Researcher
25. Sewing clothes/alterations
26. Technical writer
27. Virtual assistant
28. Website design/maintenance

EXAMPLE: Helping a small business.
Many small businesses could benefit from help from someone to set up a Twitter or Facebook presence. You can advertise locally and charge by the project, and then offer to maintain for a monthly fee.

You can also be the local expert, perhaps teaching someone to knit, or helping with technical skills such as using computer software. You can advertise locally and charge by the hour and let all your friends know exactly what you can offer. Don't forget to tell people from your church, gym, people you meet in the supermarket queue, everyone.

There are many sites that offer a wide variety of freelance work such as www.upwork.com, www.guru.com and www.peopleperhour.com/freelance/uk. See a more extensive list in Appendix 2. These are international sites so you will be competing with people who offer very low prices. But not everyone makes a decision on price alone.

You will need a professional bio and professional picture. Write in a friendly style and when you bid for work make it pertinent to the job ad; many/most will send a generic reply to everyone. Stand out by making a personalised response that addresses the requirements.

In most cases you post your details and wait for a potential employer to contact you, or you can bid for work. Read each site carefully so you understand the process, and give consideration to the fee you will quote. Set your fees slightly below the competition till you build up a reputation and get some good feedback.

Payment is easy. The employer pays the money at the start into an escrow (holding) account and when you complete the work you get paid.

When you need a survival job

You may know the job you seek, but appreciate that it may take a few months to get a job offer. Yet you need money now, **you need a survival job**, a temporary measure to bring money in. Here are some suggestions of work you could undertake which would still give you free time to job hunt. See also the list of freelance suggestions above.

- If you want to temp, rather than go through an agency you could create a flyer and spend a day distributing it in office buildings, etc. Contact small companies/retail where the owner makes the decision and *not* corporate HR.
- Consider working in a call centre. There is often a high turnover and with 24/7 shifts it can often leave you free to go to interviews during the day. Again, make a direct approach. Telemarketing companies usually have vacancies. You may not like it, but it will pay the bills and give you very useful skills – dealing with rejection/building relationships fast!
- Offer a service on www.fiverr.com.
- Look on Craigslist. In the UK lists and jobs are available for a number of different locations. Use this style of address to get to the right section – http://bristol.craigslist.co.uk.

IN A NUTSHELL

We've looked at other ways to find work including self-employment, consultancy, interim management, portfolio working and 30 ideas for earning money.

The future will be more freelance working and less full-time employment, so we need to accept this change.

BEFORE YOU MOVE ON

- Make a note of three key points you have learnt.
- Make a note of what is the top takeaway, for you, from this chapter.

- **Which of these ideas do you want to explore further? Do you want to make a plan for how to generate income as your own boss?**

14 INTERVIEWS AT 50+

The work you have done in earlier chapters should lead to interviews. This chapter will focus on specific advice for people like us, and how we can address questions around our age alongside more traditional interview advice.

The guidance will also help with informal meetings as part of your research and also for any direct approaches you make.

In this chapter you will learn:

- a general approach to answering interview questions

- specific advice for answering questions related to our age

- underlying beliefs the younger interviewer won't mention

- the importance of first impressions

- how to mentally prepare

- the need for a 90-day plan

- how to relate to a younger interviewer

- the importance of follow up.

Everything you have done so far has got you to interview. You now want to go into the interview with confidence that you can do the job and have planned how to answer both direct and indirect questions that relate to your age. You've probably already got a book to help with interview techniques, so I'm focused on specific advice for people of our age.

You may face a number of interviews; no longer is it just a first and second interview – you could well face five or more, as employers want to make sure that they have made the right decision.

I'm concentrating on traditional interviews but you may also face phone interviews and a full assessment centre selection process. You can read more on both in my book *Now you've been Shortlisted*.

Typical interview questions

Competency-based interview questions
Competency-based interviews are very popular, based on the premise that past experience is a good indicator of future performance. People of all ages struggle with this style of questioning – they give general and vague answers. As an interviewer I want a specific example and it can help to follow the **CAR** structure to focus your answer.

Here's an example of a response that uses this method to address an employer's question.

'Tell me about a time when you had to make a difficult decision.'

This is an opportunity to highlight your decision-making ability and show your thought process in coming to that decision.

The Challenge you faced:
'One of the most difficult decisions I have had to make was to choose who to give a temporary promotion to. One of the people who worked for me used to be my colleague before I received a promotion. I moved into management and we remained friends. I knew he wanted the temporary promotion but I also knew that another person was much more suited to the job in terms of experience and personality.'

The Actions you took and why:

'I knew the objective decision was not to offer the promotion to my friend but I didn't want it to lead to bad feelings. So I arranged to meet him for coffee outside of the workplace and explained my decision. I listened to what he had to say and then made some suggestions for how he could develop himself for future opportunities.'

The Results of your actions:

'The outcome was that he remained an effective employee and I made the best decision in terms of who to promote.'

We covered answering this type of question on an application form in Chapter 12, Traditional job search, so you may like to re-read that section. If you received a list of competences to use in your application be ready to discuss these again, but you may also be asked for a second example. You can draw on examples from both your work and non-work life. If you have been out of work, you may be able to refer to some voluntary work.

In particular, have examples ready to discuss that relate to:

- working with challenging people
- dealing with setbacks
- working under pressure
- solving a problem.

At non-competency-based interviews, an interviewer may start by asking you:

'Tell me about yourself.' Or 'Talk me through your career to date.'

It can take a few seconds to tune into someone's accent and voice tone so start with something like *'As you will have seen in my CV ...'* before you provide a short summary of yourself and your achievements. This may differ depending on the particular job you are applying for.

There's a tendency to start way back. Focus on the last ten years and concentrate on what is most relevant to the job you are applying for, specific achievements and skills gained. End with a question such as *'Would you like me to go into any more detail on any of this?'*

'Why do you want to work for us?'

You may be happy with _any_ job but the interviewer wants to know specifically _why_ this job and _why_ this organisation. Focus much more on what you can contribute, rather than how the job will benefit you. Show that you have done your research; explain what you have found and why it interests you. As part of your preparation you should be ready to discuss the three reasons why you are a good fit; reviewing Chapter 4 should help.

Let's now look at some questions more likely to be asked of people like us.

Questions aimed at 50+ candidates

At interview remember how you felt being interviewed by someone much older than you and how you would have wanted to be treated. Your interviewer may be nervous and may have many preconceived views on you.

In your answers choose examples where you have worked with younger people on an equal basis and/or you had a younger manager.

'You seem overqualified for this role.'

If we are applying for more junior positions we may be questioned as to why we want to take a step back, but being overqualified shouldn't be a problem. Qualification to do a job is based on competence and motivation so be ready at interview to demonstrate both. The reason this can be seen as a problem taps into some of the other questions:

- your manager will find it hard to manage you, as you are older and more experienced than him/her
- we won't be challenged and will quickly become bored by the job
- we will move on if we get a better offer
- we will expect a higher salary than is budgeted
- it will be a comedown and we won't adapt well to taking orders.

Your answer may include a bit of a white lie. You may need to say that you are no longer interested in climbing the career ladder, you want to move to a role where your experience is valuable and you can use your expertise and experience. Emphasise how much you enjoy this type of work. A good answer could be:

'While I'll still give 100% when I'm on the job, I've decided that at this stage of life I want the flexibility to be able to spend more time with my family. Therefore I'm interested in this role …'

OR

'I'm interested in a return to a more customer-facing role because that is the position I found most satisfying.'

'Most of the staff are in their twenties and thirties. How do you think you will fit in?'
The interviewer is worried that you will find it hard to relate to younger people, but also that you will have a negative impact on the team, making them feel like their mum or dad is in the room. Have examples that you can share of how you have worked effectively with people of different ages. Emphasise how you enjoy the mentoring aspect of working with younger colleagues. But also how much you have learnt from younger colleagues – a bit like reverse-mentoring. You may like to say that you have friends of different ages. You could also say that you may be able to provide a different perspective, which is helpful, rather than having a workforce which is too similar in background.

Coming across as lively and energetic and open in body language and style will help, as too will be using the language and style on your CV that resonates with 20- and 30-year-olds.

'The manager is aged 30, will that be a problem to you?'
Some people find it difficult to accept direction from someone the age of their son or daughter. If that's you, you have to get over this, it's *your* problem. You must demonstrate that you are able to take direction, and are open to constructive criticism. Again, talk about working with people from a wide range of ages and how you are always open to learning new ways of doing a task and working as part of an energetic and enthusiastic group.

'Aren't you getting ready to retire?'
I think this is to get at a perceived lack of energy and I'm not sure anyone will come directly out with asking this question, but if they do, address it straight

on. Tell them that you enjoy working, that you have a lot to offer and expect to be working for at least the next ten years.

At interview and when we meet with people we can talk about our active hobbies such as dancing and hiking. We can talk about the classes we have taken, the TED talks we love, all will show us as someone with energy. Explain how you enjoy sharing knowledge, learning and making a contribution.

Preconceived ideas

Not everything is asked as a question; there may be underlying views that we need to address. Many younger interviewers, and the workforce in general, have certain beliefs. Let's address seven of the most pervasive ones.

1. We cost too much

Many employers think we won't take a drop in salary, so at interview you can say that money isn't the key driver and is a secondary consideration. I know that you may really need to maintain your salary level, but you may prefer to come across as someone for whom money is not the key decider. A good response could be:

'I'm comfortable with accepting a lower salary if it means doing work that is meaningful to me.' OR
'I'm fortunate that now I've cleared my mortgage I can choose the work I want to do rather than focus on salary.'

You need to be realistic about the salary range for the job, but there is usually a range and you can demonstrate your value so you get an offer at the top end of the salary band.

2. We are resistant to change and inflexible

Some people are; they want things done the way they always have. Others are far too cautious to try anything new. We can address this through being active in social media, hence almost all 50+ job-seekers need to use LinkedIn effectively. We also need to show enthusiasm to learn new things.

Don't just tell interviewers that you are flexible, have examples ready to share about how you have collaboratively solved problems and anything new you have recently got involved with.

3. We cannot or will not learn new skills

I regularly meet people who rest on the skills and qualifications gained 20+ years ago and do the minimum of professional development. In many jobs you need to demonstrate proficiency, confirmed through completing a course or through some other type of learning.

If you've been away from a full-time job for a year, what do you need to do to make sure that your skills are up to date? Do you need to undertake a short course in using Excel? Are you familiar with the latest version of Office used in the workplace?

On your CV you should have a section called professional development, not just education, and include examples of how you are keeping your skills and knowledge up to date. Be ready at interview to refer to what you have recently read in the business pages of a newspaper and professional journals such as *The Grocer*.

It's not just about work-related learning. You can be ready to discuss how you have e.g. recently started dance classes or are learning a foreign language or to program using Raspberry Pi.

4. We aren't up to date with technology

There is a massive misconception that because we are 50+ we don't do technology. You may well be like many of my friends who started working with PCs back in the 1980s and have a substantial underlying knowledge of technology from the days of DOS.

Mature workers are the fastest-growing users of technology, but not all are; some people have never had to use computers in their work and lack confidence. If you lack confidence you can attend a course or perhaps get a younger relative or college student to provide some one-to-one tuition.

I've written before about self-talk: see Chapter 2. If you keep telling yourself that you don't do technology, it is not helping you to get into the right state to learn.

You need to understand about the different types of social media – LinkedIn, Twitter, and Pinterest. Apart from LinkedIn (and you should have a link to this from your CV) you don't need to set up your own account but you need to understand what they are and use e.g. Twitter as part of your research. In our interview answers we can demonstrate our knowledge through referring to an article on the employer's Twitter feed.

5. We lack energy and enthusiasm

Some employers think we won't have the energy for a fast-paced environment. We can demonstrate our energy through our body language (look alert, sit up and speak with energy) and appearance, such as a more youthful haircut. We can also make sure that we have underlying fitness through regular exercise and that we eat and sleep well.

We must show enthusiasm. If we don't have much of this for our job search it's going to be a major barrier to success. People want to work with people who enjoy the work they do and are interested in the subject. Talk less about your years of experience and more about what you still want to achieve. Remember how enthusiastic you were at the start of your career – make sure you still have that enthusiasm and it comes through. Let your interviewer know why you are excited about this opportunity and what you can bring to the company.

We need to make sure we also look energetic and need to consider our clothes, haircut and accessories. They should have at least a nod to what's in fashion, so look at current magazines and high-street stores. It will help us to promote a confident image and we also need to make sure that we look active and vital. Wendy was quite proud of her interview outfit and said it was from the 1980s. Yes – I wore padded shoulders too, 30 years ago! The look dated her. She looked much better when she bought a different outfit from a high-street fashion store.

6. We have health problems – we take more time off sick

Some people of all ages can have health problems. If you do, you don't need to refer to it unless they ask how much time you have taken off sick in the past year.

From mid-life we often concentrate on improving our health, we eat better, drink less, and mature workers are the least-likely group to take days off due to illness. Address their concerns by talking about your active lifestyle which helps demonstrate that we are staying fit and healthy. Look for a chance to say that e.g. you haven't taken a day off sick for three years.

7. We don't need the money

What a generalisation! Not everyone has retired early with lots of money in the bank. Many, many people are still in need of a salary to enable them to pay the bills. The focus should be on your contribution and how you can help the organisation to solve problems, achieve goals and make or save money.

Key points

At interview we should emphasise how much we are interested in this opportunity and explain why the job interests us.

If we aren't asked the questions referred to earlier which could cover concerns about our age we can address them by looking for a chance to:

- address the issue that we may be seen as too expensive
- address the issue that our experience will be a hindrance rather than an asset. An interviewer may believe your work style will be a carry-over from your previous positions rather than learning their approach. Explain that you love to learn new things
- say you will be comfortable being managed by someone younger than yourself.

Even if it isn't true you can say that salary is not the main driver, it is the interesting work, and that you are in a position where you can choose meaningful work over salary.

Focus on the advantages to the employer. You have the experience to make an immediate impact right away. You have a wide network of contacts that you can draw on. You can informally mentor younger members of staff. Have stories ready to share.

Interview practice

START PRACTISING

You could use an interview coach, or you can role-play with a friend who can ask you questions. Ask your friend to give you feedback on what you did well and how you can improve. Ask them to comment on your body language and tone; it's not just what you say but how you say it. You can also practise in front of a mirror, to see how your smile, etc. comes across.

As you plan how you will answer questions, always say your answers out loud, don't rely on what you hear in your head. (We always sound better in our head!) If you record your answers, you will be able to review how you sound, your level of energy, and you will notice the number of times you say 'you know', etc.

As an interviewer, I expect my candidates to be well prepared with examples for most of the questions I ask, and that they will ask me intelligent questions which demonstrate they have thought about the role and how they would be successful if they were offered the job.

First impressions
It's highly likely the interviewer will be younger, perhaps much younger than us. Think of it from their viewpoint, especially if your CV gives the impression of you being 10–15 years younger than you are. What would you think when a much older person walks through the door?

So walk in with confidence, and a bounce to your step, be ready to address negative stereotypes and the early advice will help.

Throughout make sure you show passion and enthusiasm – this is an area where too many people of our age let ourselves down. Our voice can be flat, we come across as 'going through the motions'. Put some enthusiasm into your answers and also make sure you come across as passionate about the company and the industry.

Get yourself ready

Re-read your CV and cover letter or application, plus the job ad and any supporting information, and be 100% certain you can back up every claim with a specific and detailed answer.

Think about any areas where you know you are weaker. What can you say to compensate for any perceived weakness? But also, you may have something extra that you can offer – experience of a particular situation such as dealing with exports to China, when you've read they've got their first order into this emerging market. This may be beneficial to your role so be sure to be ready to let them know.

Of course you will have looked at the company website, but also have a view on its competitors and industry developments, and know what is happening right now through a news search in the business press and from comments on public sites. You will gain a competitive edge if you can demonstrate your knowledge of the industry you are applying to, not just knowledge of the role you have applied for.

Keeping up to date on news about the organisation means that you can be ready with some extra evidence to support your application.

Mental preparation

Just like a sportsperson, you must prepare mentally. Imagine every element of the interview and possible problems that you may be asked to address, and prepare a reply. This should include the emotional, feeling element. This will make it much easier for you to be effective on the day.

Do you get anxious before interviews? Interviewers can sense it when they speak to you. You may find it helps to spend time performing meditation and relaxation practices to improve your job search conversations, and to appear more confident.

Think yourself to success at interview

As part of your preparation for interview, you will be practising interview questions, sorting out your interview clothes – but how much time do you spend on developing a positive attitude? Read again Chapter 2, Mindset and think about your inner talk. Stop making negative comments, and for the interview swap these for statements such as the following.

- *'This is going to be a really interesting interview.'*
- *'I'm looking forward to talking about my experience.'*
- *'I want to learn more about the company.'*
- *'I will be fine regardless of whether I get the job or not.'*

This will help you be calmer and enable you to focus on your strengths.

It can be easy for negative thoughts to come into your head during the interview – 'I'm too old for the job', 'I rambled through that answer', 'What if I don't get the job?' but this distracts you from doing your best, so as these thoughts come into your head, blow them away! Take deep breaths and stay calm.

Over to you – questions to ask at the end of the interview
At the end of the interview, you will be asked if you have any questions. So many of the people I interview mumble about everything having been covered. It makes for a weak ending. The best candidates open their briefcase, pull out a pad with a few questions listed and choose three or four to ask.

Your research will have identified why you will be a great candidate. Prepare a question you could ask at interview which would allow you to use a particular achievement as an illustration. You can do this for all of your strengths – this will mean you not only have great examples ready to use in answer to every question, but you can also ask questions of your own that reinforce your strengths. An example might be: 'Is there a need to simplify processes? I'm asking because when I was in my last job I introduced processing mapping, which resulted in savings of time and increased effectiveness.'

You could also ask the following questions.

- *Since the job was advertised, have your requirements been amended?*
- *Why are you going outside of the company?*
- *Who would I be replacing? Why is that person leaving?*
- *What would you see as my priorities in this job?*
- *If I were to be offered the job, what preparation could I do?*
- *I am very interested in this job and believe I can do it well; do you have any concerns about me as a candidate?*

Preparing a 90-day plan

The first 90 days in a job are crucial. Some employers are asking for a 30/60/90-day plan as part of a more thorough selection and new-hire process. I think this will become more popular, so anticipate.

Let an employer know what you will do through creating and taking along a 90-day plan. Think of yourself as successful in the job. You would want to know the department's goals and objectives. Ask questions at interview, or through meetings with people to answer this question. What specifically would you need to achieve. What will be your priorities? How does your job fit into the broader organisational goals? Which are the top priorities and why?

Who do you need to meet and build relationships with? Who holds the informal power? You want to know the people in your department but also key people who you will come into contact with. What will be a quick win, what can be completed quickly to improve an aspect of the department or company? You would talk to stakeholders to get their input.

A first interview, along with your research, should help you to construct a plan that you can take along at further interviews.

The day of the interview

When you arrive

Aim to arrive five to ten minutes early to allow time to check your appearance in the mirror. Putting your phone on silent might be enough but as you don't want it to vibrate, it's probably best to play safe and switch it off. You may be kept waiting so bring something to read.

Be in a positive frame of mind

You may or may not feel confident but for the interview, you must portray a positive image. There's some research that says smiling can help make you feel happy. So put on a big smile and keep your eyes smiling afterwards.

Interviewers will often seek a general view on candidates from administrators, so be friendly and positive with everyone you meet. You know you will have to shake hands so have a firm handshake, and use antiperspirant if you have a tendency to sweaty hands.

At the interview

You only have one chance to make a first impression. Put into practice the techniques of relaxation and alertness. Make sure you breathe and listen. Be confident in your ability and how you will behave. Also be assertive: if, for example, you have the sun in your eyes, ask for the blinds to be dropped or to move your chair.

It's against the law to ask questions about age in an interview, but more subtle signs of ageism can creep into the verbal exchange, so answer questions carefully and with energy.

Many interviewers make up their minds about a candidate within seconds of meeting them. This is known as the 'halo effect'. When we observe one good thing about someone, we assume all kinds of other good things about the person. It's not fair, but we do it anyway. For example, if you are well dressed, many interviewers will assume you are probably responsible in other ways.

With the 'halo effect' the interviewer is subconsciously seeking to have that initial favourable impression confirmed by the subsequent discussion. The opposite is the 'horns effect'. If you start off badly, perhaps by the way you are dressed, your clammy hands or tripping up as you go into the interview room, you'll have an uphill struggle for the rest of the interview.

You can make the interviewer feel good right from the start. As you are greeted by them, you could say, 'I just want to let you know how much I appreciate you meeting with me. This position sounds exciting and I've heard nothing but good things about (company name).'

Expect to get on with your interviewer, and show you do through your verbal and non-verbal behaviour.

Use your body language to good effect: use hand gestures to emphasise a point – but not too much – and make eye contact. Too many people look shifty, as they don't want to look at the person interviewing them. If you find it hard to look directly at someone, imagine you are looking at a triangle made up of their eyes and nose.

Demonstrating confidence means that you will stand, sit, and walk with good posture and confidence. You will have a firm and decisive handshake, call the interviewer by his or her name, and say how pleased you are to be there (and mean it!).

Speak loudly and clearly enough to be heard. Make sure you stress your good points and show how well informed you are about the organisation. Keep your attitude businesslike and respectful. Sell yourself by giving solid reasons **why** you want to work for the company and showing **how** you can help them.

Make sure you recount things in an interesting and positive way so that the interviewer will remember you. Listen closely as the interviewers introduce themselves. You should try to address them by name at another point during the interview.

Be natural, relaxed and enthusiastic. Remember, you are already more than halfway to the job. You are at interview because the selectors consider you can do the job. Be self-assured, but not over-confident, overbearing or arrogant. Show your passion. **If there are two equally qualified candidates, the more passionate one will likely get the job.**

Think before you talk. Take a few seconds to collect and organise your thoughts, and then answer each question simply and directly. If you do not understand the question or the motivation behind it, ask for clarification. Use jargon or technical terms only if you fully understand them and if they will help to show your knowledge of a subject.

Answering questions

Before you start to answer a question, in your head say to yourself, 'I need to answer this question in a way that will show how I can be of value to this employer.' If you start to ramble, interrupt yourself by coughing or pausing. This will give you time to collect your thoughts and you can say 'Sorry, can I start that answer again?'

As you cover them at interview, mentally tick off the five or six key reasons why you should be considered for the job. Find opportunities to raise any topics which have not been covered. You might be asked whether you would like to add anything or you might make the point yourself: 'Would it be helpful if I mentioned something else relevant to this job?' Take every opportunity to explain your achievements and abilities within the context of the job description.

Never hesitate to ask the interviewer to repeat the question if you haven't fully heard or understood it. You can also use the technique of restating the question in different words to check your understanding.

Let the interviewer control the interview, but always be prepared to take the initiative. Have a strategy for handling interviewers who monopolise the talking, or ask only closed ('Yes/No') questions. Be prepared for the deliberate question which the interviewer knows you cannot answer. Such questions are useful to interviewers as much to see how you will cope as for the content of your reply.

If the interviewer starts asking questions where you need to imagine yourself in the role, for example, asking you 'How would you handle …?' it is helpful to pretend that you are not being interviewed for a job. Instead, imagine you are a respected consultant helping a new client with a problem. Adopt a probing approach so that you can understand their situation in sufficient detail before providing an answer. Relate your answer to their business objectives rather than to theories or models (unless specifically asked to do so).

Similarly, when asked about your past achievements, relate them to issues your employer was trying to address and the business (organisational) benefits they gained. This way, you will be giving very useful examples, and, by not trying to 'perform', you will be more relaxed. It is useful to remind yourself of the following:

- **Keep on your toes.** Everyone feels nervous before an interview; this is quite natural. Butterflies in the stomach are caused by the same surge of adrenaline that an athlete gets before an important race. It's the body's way of tuning up your faculties for peak performance. Channel this energy by keeping super-alert and notice the interviewer's body language for clues on how much detail you should be giving them. For example, do they appear attentive or bored?
- **Build rapport.** The interview is also about what you are like to work with. Hence, building rapport may be as important as impressing with expertise.
- **Give careful consideration to all your answers.** Don't be afraid to pause and think before replying to a question, and don't hesitate to say you don't know if that is the case (but not too often!).

- **Focus on your plusses.** I encourage my clients to focus on accomplishments, how they have learnt, how they best solve problems and techniques to help them achieve with less chance of getting distracted.
- **Be natural.** Wanting to give your best doesn't mean that you have to be unnatural. High anxiety about the outcome can lead us to either try too hard or come over as dull and stilted. Aim to strike a balance between being comfortable and relaxed and alert and incisive.
- **Be positive.** Don't criticise previous employers, as you'll project a negative image of yourself. On the other hand, if you have made a mistake in your career, it is not a disaster to admit it, but make sure you convey clearly the lessons it taught you. Admitting the odd mistake also gives you credibility when you start to talk about the positive things in your career.

Your questions

Have prepared questions written down; you don't need to commit them to memory. Open your folder and read them out. Ask a question to identify some of the organisation's problems. You can then focus your thank-you letter on addressing these issues and use them in the 30/60/90-day plan.

A perfect close

Once you have asked your questions, you have a final chance to make a positive impression. You can now make a one-minute closing statement. Summarise your qualifications, skills and accomplishments and emphasise your interest in the job. Thank the interviewer, and be sure to ask about the next step or stage. Make sure you say goodbye to the receptionist as you leave.

Post-interview evaluation

As soon as you can, jot down a few notes, outlining the main points discussed. Complete a review of how you think you came across. It will be invaluable to refer to if you get a second interview and you can also use it to monitor your performance. Be honest with yourself, noting what you did well, and where improvements are needed. Talk through the result of your review with a friend and practise your revised answers.

There are many questions you can ask yourself, such as the following.

- Was I in the right frame of mind?
- Was my eye contact right? Did I smile?

- Was there anything I should have known about the company that I did not?
- How effective was my role in the interview?
- Which questions did I handle well? Which questions did I handle poorly?
- How well did I ask questions? What could I have done differently?
- Did I appear confident and show genuine enthusiasm?
- Did I talk too much?
- Did I give answers which didn't seem to satisfy the interviewer?
- Was I able to discuss my strengths and weaknesses?
- Did I find out all I needed to?
- Would I like to work for that organisation?

Follow up with a thank-you letter

Very few candidates write a follow-up letter. If the interviewer is undecided this may just tip the balance in your favour. The purpose of your thank-you letter is to reinforce your strengths, experience and accomplishments. Include anything that relates to and expands on what was discussed at interview. It is not just to thank them for their time.

Your thank-you letter can address areas of weakness, and any reservations or concerns that were mentioned during the interview. You can also explain how your strengths and past work history (with examples) can over-compensate for any areas of weakness.

Most importantly, you will provide brief details of how you can solve the recruiter's problem. But you don't want to tell them everything – you want them to get back in touch with you.

A sample letter

> *Thank you for the opportunity to interview with you last Tuesday for the position of business development manager. During the interview you asked why I was a good candidate and my response was a little vague. I am a good candidate because...*
>
> *You also said that one of the problems you have is XXX. I've been thinking of ways to solve this and would love an opportunity to discuss my ideas further. I have identified one area in particular...'*

… And then you explain what you would do to solve the problem, but not how you would do it – that's what you want to discuss with them at a second interview.

It's better to email the thank-you note because decisions may be made quickly, but a handwritten note has greater impact.

Further (second and third) interviews
You will need to do some extra research for subsequent interviews, but don't forget to review your notes from the first one. The more knowledgeable you are in advance, the more effective you will be. Remember that everyone you meet is evaluating you, just as you are evaluating them. Always ask about the next steps after the interview and when you will hear from them. Then make a diary note to get in touch the day after.

The interview could have even more rounds – having in excess of ten interviews for one job can happen – so ask about the process and never think you have the job in the bag.

If you don't get the job

In some cases it will be expected. In your post-interview review you will have identified where you could have done better, and can use this learning for next time. In other cases you may not be able to identify anything wrong. You may have done a brilliant interview and still not have been offered the job. You may have a strong suspicion of ageism; you may be right.

It could be that there was more than one person who was capable of doing the job and the final decision may have been based on factors outside your control. The person who got the job may have been an internal candidate or had something extra to offer. Or there may never have been a job available. The head office may have wanted to fill the vacancy but the job had already been offered to someone, and the whole interview process was a sham.

Whatever you think is the reason you didn't get the job, contact the organisation and ask for feedback. Even if you do not get an offer, you can still write one last letter. The person who has been offered the job may turn it down. Quite regularly, a new employee leaves fairly quickly as it hasn't worked out for them. Your letter could bring you to the top of the list when a new person is being considered.

IN A NUTSHELL

Getting shortlisted is only half the battle; we need to convince at interview that we can do the job, and show age as an asset.

This chapter has addressed many of the questions, and you need to practise answering them so you feel relaxed.

Focus too on your mindset: it's how we feel that can have a significant impact on our success or lack of it.

Practise answering questions and continue to seek out good examples to share at interview. Especially follow the competency-based format of CAR.

ACTIVITY 35

BEFORE YOU MOVE ON

- Make a note of three key points you have learnt.
- Make a note of what is the top takeaway, for you, from this chapter.

15 STAYING MOTIVATED

Keeping our motivation high can be hard at all ages. If you find your motivation slipping, first go back and re-read Chapter 2, Mindset. Then read on for some helpful action you can take to keep going.

In this chapter we will discuss:

■ techniques to help you deal with rejection

■ the need for mental toughness

■ the importance of self-talk to increase self-confidence

■ the power of our thoughts

■ taking a more positive outlook

■ ten ways to improve motivation

■ the need to measure progress.

Y ou will get setbacks and knockbacks, so you need to be ready for them. There are many reasons apart from age as to why we may not get shortlisted or succeed at interview. Many times shortlisting has been done by a computer system; at interview there can be many people who could do the job equally well.

Dealing with rejection

What we can do is to review everything we are doing to see how we can improve. We may think we have a great CV, but if it is not getting us to interview, it is not doing its job. It may be that you need to create a more focused CV and cover letter, or you may need to spend more time on research – re-read the advice in earlier chapters. If necessary, seek an independent job-search coach to provide feedback and guidance to help you improve.

You may think you interview well, but carrying out a full interview with an experienced interviewer who coaches you is worth the investment. The relevant chapters in this book tell you how to conduct yourself at interview, and practice sessions with a friend may help you improve, but you may still benefit from exploring other subtleties with an experienced interviewer.

Keep a positive attitude

Professional Advice

Whether you think you can or you can't, you're right.

Henry Ford, Founder, Ford Motor Company

You need a positive attitude: you need to believe that you can do something, that you can achieve your goal. You could find inspiration through books and reading other people's success stories and re-read Chapter 2, Mindset.

The need for mental toughness

It is not just about having a positive mental attitude, it's also dealing with setbacks. Like a footballer who misses a pass, a focus on the failure will impact throughout the rest of the game. They have to put their mistake(s) behind them and refocus. They and you need to demonstrate mental toughness which includes:

■ **self-belief** – confidence in your skills and abilities
■ **motivation** – to keep applying till you get interviewed, and continue despite rejections

- **focus** – on what you need to do to get a job, to ace the interview and later focus on what is going right, not what's going wrong
- **composure** – to stay calm during the stress of an interview.

Confidence and self-talk

Self-talk

Use much more positive self-talk. Before an interview you can say things like, *'My body is relaxed and I feel confident.'* During an interview you can say to yourself, *'I'm calm and in control, I'm speaking clearly and have great examples to share.'* After an interview you can say, *'I'm doing well, I've learnt more about interviews to help me for next time.'* While you wait to hear the outcome of an interview, you can say, *'I am a worthwhile person and the right job is out there.'*

Negative self-talk can really hamper our chance of a new job. If we ask ourselves, 'Why can't I get a job?' our brains will focus on all the reasons why we can't get one – we are too old, too fat or too short, have too much experience or not enough. We need to get our subconscious minds working on a different question, something like *'What can I do to get this job?'* or *'How can I show an employer that I'm the right person for this job?'*

Stop saying 'I can't get a job'; change it to *'I will get a job'*. Stop saying you are useless and remind yourself that you are doing something useful each day. Don't say you are too old, say that you are the right age for a new opportunity.

If we expect to be unsuccessful in meetings and at interview, then we are likely to come across that way, and will be seen as someone who can't confidently discuss the great examples of their experience. However, if we think we are going to be successful and have planned how to respond to questions, we stand a much better chance.

The need for confidence

Confidence means that we have the belief that we will succeed. When we lack confidence, we set ourselves up for a negative and downward spiral. When we lack confidence, we don't perform well, our performance is more hesitant, and we are less likely to be successful, so we don't get the job and this negative feedback can affect our confidence still further.

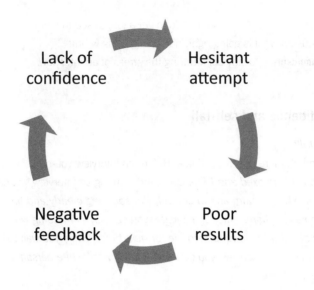

Our thought processes

What we think can have a powerful impact on our confidence. If we have negative thoughts and beliefs it can result in a downward spiral. You may hear these voices.

- **The Critic** who tells you what a disappointment you are and that if you ask for help it is a sign of weakness.
- **The Perfectionist** who tells you that you should do this and you must do that, and that you have to be perfect in everything you do, and that you must be competent at all times – it is unthinkable to fail.
- **The Worrier** who gets you to catastrophise and ask 'What if …?' questions, such as 'What if I don't get this job?' Maybe you won't, but you should learn from it and improve for next time. Catastrophising and expecting the worst doesn't help; you need to focus more on performing well.
- **The Victim** who knows that it is nothing to do with them, it's all to do with someone else. They think that nothing will make any difference and expect to fail at the interview, will tell you that no-one wants you and that you will never be able to get another job.

We must challenge these voices

We mustn't let these voices take over. Stop saying 'No-one ever responds to my job applications' – really? No-one? Stop thinking that people are out to get you.

Many people apply for jobs and not getting shortlisted can be down to many reasons outside your control.

We need to hear different voices, the ones that tell us that we are on track and to focus much more on the positive. Instead of thinking of disappointments we need to think of our successes and remind ourselves of situations we handled well, times when people praised and thanked us, and so on.

The impact on others

Feel sorry for yourself and you will feel like a victim; spend too much time moaning and people won't want to be around you. Look for ways to remain interesting and to keep friendships and relationships going.

Quit, just for a while

If you are getting down, you could give yourself a job-search holiday: take some time out and take your CV down from all the job sites. Check that you still want to aim for the job you have been seeking. Get someone to provide a critical review of your CV, make any changes, and then start afresh. Go back to the section on affirmations in Chapter 2.

Ten ways to improve motivation

1. Visualise yourself succeeding

We covered this in Chapter 2 where I asked you to imagine yourself being successful in your job search. It is a powerful technique and you should go back and read this section.

You can't be in a happy and an unhappy mood at the same time. Changing your posture and facial expression can help. Put on a happy face and keep saying, 'I feel happy, I feel healthy, and I feel terrific.'

2. Remind yourself of previous successes

Can you remember a time when you won a race, created a great report, made a presentation that convinced your boss to go ahead with a project or to give you a rise? Now is the time to remind yourself of previous successes. You might like to buy a notebook and write them down as you remember them. You've been successful before and you will be again. **Re-read your CV each day to remind yourself of your achievements and what a great job you did.**

3. Remember – not everything is down to you

Remind yourself that it's not all within your control. You can have a great CV, interview well and look great but still find yourself unemployed and waiting for a job offer. Many people find themselves in this position. So keep doing the best you can and don't take your lack of a job offer too personally. Not getting a job does not mean that you are not a wonderful person, and you should look for as many ways as you can to keep your spirits high.

4. Avoid negative people

Some people love to be negative, to see the world as a half-empty glass, to complain, to see problems, to expect to fail. Spend too much time with people like this and you are likely to start thinking the same way. Who do you know that will inspire you and keep you feeling positive? You need to spend more time with people like that! Perhaps you should look to broaden the circle of people you know and meet more positive people. Perhaps joining a book group or a walking group would help. Find out details of groups local to you through Meetup.com.

Richard thought this was great advice and was eager to see what groups he could join.

5. Focus on your goal

Make sure you are clear on the job you want and why. It may help to return to some of the earlier chapters in the book. Are you clear on the job you want, location, and why you should get the job?

6. Get out from behind your computer and connect with more people

Have you slipped into old habits of looking for jobs online? Just using the internet will not help, and browsing through job boards can lead to feelings of overwhelm. Get out there and talk with people.

Of course, these conversations will help you reach your job-hunting goals but sometimes doing something less focused on your job search leads to success. Perhaps talking with a neighbour and spending time listening to them could be helpful in both building your community and leading to helpful contacts.

> **Case Study**
> Valerie found that talking with a neighbour about gardening led to a subject change and the neighbour offering to get in touch with their niece who worked in insurance.

Have you reconnected with people from your past, and people you know, especially local people if you want to get a job in the local area? Today on a Facebook page for my local area someone asked about getting a job and got seven suggestions of local companies who needed staff. Use the power of others to help you.

7. Volunteer

Could you use some of your spare time in voluntary work? You could use the skills you already have to benefit others, or use this as an opportunity to develop new skills. You may meet people in a position to offer you a job. At the very least, you will meet people who you can add to your network. And remember, many prospective employers think highly of a person who is involved with volunteer activities, so it will enhance your CV.

The best volunteering when you are job-hunting involves doing something related to the job you seek. If you are a marketing executive, offer to create a marketing plan for a charity. This will be far more effective for your job search than volunteering to work in a charity shop or tidying a country park.

8. Get a job-search buddy

You may find your job search more fun with a buddy, who you can meet on a weekly basis to share progress. Find someone else in a similar situation to you who will help keep you motivated and with whom you can share ideas. It can also be someone who is enthusiastic and will energise you.

9. Keep learning

Learn something that will enhance your CV. It doesn't have to be an expensive course; there are lots of training opportunities available for free. You may not be able to gain a qualification but you can still learn new skills. How can you improve – what can you do today to make a difference? Read articles, watch TED talks. More on this in Chapter 16, How to stay employable.

It doesn't just have to be about the job; you could also learn to play a musical instrument, write a short story, and train for a half marathon.

10. Read motivational books

Keep yourself inspired during your job search. Read blogs by people you find inspiring such as Anthony Robbins and Zen Habits.

And get mentally ready. Get those endorphins released. Stand up and close your eyes. Imagine anything that makes you happy, such as success in your job hunt. Then imagine you are successful and enjoying the success. Do this every day.

Measure your progress

When trying to lose weight we set targets for how many calories to eat and how many steps to walk, or times to visit the gym. You need to follow a plan to include how many people you will contact each day, and to follow up 100% on every letter you send.

Sometimes we think that nothing is happening – no-one has come back to us to suggest a job, but people will know what you seek and with consistent action things should improve. But you must stay focused.

We can often think we are doing the right things, but over the weeks we deviate and get a little off-plan, so it will help to keep focused on your plan.

You may be seeking to do anything rather than having to complete another application form or to revise your CV. Rather than seeing this as a chore you can focus more on how great you will feel as you submit another application that is highly targeted to the job you want.

ACTIVITY 36

MOTIVATION MEASUREMENT

- On a scale of 1–10 how motivated are you feeling right now?
- And how motivated did you think you were at the start of this book?
- Measure how you feel each week, and if your motivation drops take action – talk to someone inspiring, read some articles, get out and meet new people.

IN A NUTSHELL

The chapter has provided you with many hints and tips to help increase your motivation. Some of the techniques will resonate more with you, so make a plan of three things you can do to help with motivation when you feel yourself feeling a bit down.

I've also raised the importance of measuring your progress. Look how far you have come and celebrate small improvements.

BEFORE YOU MOVE ON

- Make a note of three key points you have learnt.
- Make a note of what is the top takeaway, for you, from this chapter.

- **Diarise to measure your levels of motivation each week, just like a weekly weigh-in.**

16 HOW TO STAY EMPLOYABLE

One reason job-seekers aged 50+ struggle is due to their professional expertise being dated and not having professional qualifications.

In this chapter I'm going to:

- make a case for taking ownership of your development

- discuss different learning options – it's not just going on courses

- explain why it helps to understand your learning style

- suggest where to find online courses

- explain that voluntary work can also be a great way to develop new skills.

We need to stand up against prejudice and ageism. We also need to challenge ourselves to keep our knowledge up to date and to take responsibility for self-development, not leave it to our employer.

Take ownership of your development

Employees are now often seen as commodities and thus our company may be less likely to invest in us. We are paid for a set of skills, and keeping our skills current is now down to us as individuals.

As a psychologist and careers professional I attend courses, and read voraciously to keep up to date. But not everyone does. People will wait for their boss to put them on a training course. This may not happen, partly down to lack of budget but also because others may have preconceived ideas that we aren't interested in a course.

But some people have never been offered training. Simon had no development as a postman. Was it assumed that because of his type of work that he wasn't going to be receptive to learning? A terribly condescending attitude, perhaps. In his spare time he devoured history books and people assumed he was a history teacher. Maybe he could have been, but his work with museum outreach drew on this personal development.

The National Careers Service offers Lifelong Learning Accounts and you may like to set one up.

A lack of training can cost you a job

Leo was a marketing director, and at 53 was made redundant. He assumed it would be easy to get another job, but wasn't getting shortlisted. By the time he'd come to see me his confidence had dropped. It was hard to give him the news that without membership of the Chartered Institute of Marketers he was going to find it hard to get shortlisted.

Keeping up to date

It's not just psychologists like me who need to stay up to date. In all industries we can keep current on news in our industry or sector. Be sure to read the business pages and industry magazines, such as *Accountacy Age* or *The Caterer*.

Create your own database of news sites that have relevant news. For many, this will include the *Financial Times* – it's not just for directors. As a middle-manager psychologist I used to subscribe to both the *Harvard Business Review* and *The Economist* to give me an edge over other psychologists through developing a stronger business focus.

Association membership

You may have let an industry or professional association membership lapse. It may be a good time to re-join or join as an associate member.

You can keep up with the latest trends in your field and connect with colleagues who often know about possible jobs before they are advertised. Volunteer to help out at meetings to meet a large number of members with the least amount of effort.

What learning will help you get a new job?

Let's be pragmatic: you want to make sure that any learning you undertake will increase your chance of keeping your job or getting a new one. It may be that you want to get professionally qualified, but more likely it will be shorter courses that can be seen as continuing professional development (CPD).

I find that my clients aged 50+ who are most successful in getting back into work are the ones that stay on top of the new developments in their areas of expertise and are clear on how they can add value to an employer. The people who expect their employers to take responsibility for their development, or who think they're just paid to do their job, have struggled more.

Case Study

Rachael said: 'Last night I ended up stumbling on to the AAT website, and their Twitter page, and from there to a webinar they were doing, which was empowering. I have done the first two stages, my Foundation and Intermediate. I would love to do the Technician stage at some point. This has helped me to be aware of all my options.'

Essential skills

Back in Chapter 3 you assessed yourself against a list of skills. Regularly monitor your skills and see which are in more demand and look for ways to develop. Do you need to become more proficient in using Excel, or to become more strategic?

Soft skills may also need development, so consider developing interpersonal skills, problem-solving, critical thinking, team working, and building self-confidence.

You can check on the required skills through looking at job ads and seeing what skills and certifications are required. Once you have them, make sure to list them prominently on your CV and LinkedIn profile.

Seek development opportunities at work

Many employers think that beyond a certain age we aren't interested in attending courses and other learning activities, so make it known. Volunteer to get involved in new activities and make sure your boss knows you are interested in any courses on offer.

Ask a professional colleague how you can be of help to them. By listening to their questions it can help deepen our own knowledge.

If you are out of work, find out about training options

Government training schemes – Talking with colleagues, I've found that while many government training schemes can give people something to do, they don't always lead to work. Due diligence is needed before you say yes. Apprenticeships can seem like a good option, but at present that first year of the programme pays only £2.73 per hour.

What would you like to learn? The one thing we have plenty of when out of work is time, so alongside your job search, consider what else you would like to learn – a language, DJ skills?

The benefits ... Alongside helping you, you can also include your new skills on your CV and discuss them at interview. Be ready to explain what you have gained from these experiences.

There can even be health benefits. Learning a language, for example, has been shown to delay the onset of Alzheimer's. Time for me to focus on learning Spanish!

Learning styles

We learn in different ways. How do you learn best?

- Is it through working with others in a class or a small group?
- Do you prefer to work on your own, reading and following online resources?
- Do you prefer to sit down with someone who explains everything to you and will answer your questions?
- Do you prefer to learn hands-on? To learn though trial and error?

You could complete an online assessment to help you clarify your preferred learning style, such as www.howtolearn.com/learning-styles-quiz.

Knowing this will help you to make the right choice for you.

Where to learn
Finding online short courses
There are many free and very low-cost courses available for you to take online and you may like to consider:

- TED talks
- MOOCs, The Open Education Consortium, www.oeconsortium.org/courses/, www.coursera.org – you can access hundreds of courses from universities including law, science and business strategy
- YouTube – offers a large number of instructional videos to help you learn specific skills
- edX – a particular favourite of mine – www.edx.org

In-person courses
Visit your local college to see what courses are available.

Reading
Visit your local library and look at relevant sections – business, professional, or self-help. You may also find good books in charity shops and for £0.01 on Amazon.

Podcasts
Look on iTunes and see the vast number of podcasts you can subscribe to.

Attend seminars, meetings, trade shows
When you attend relevant professional development courses, network with your fellow students to build your knowledge and connections. If you attend an online class, contact each person to network – make social media social!

When attending professional or industry conferences, look up the speaker and any attendees on a list in advance to enable you to connect with them in advance of the meeting. If you can't afford the course fee, you could volunteer – all conferences need people to work on the check-in desk and help out. Or read the literature and follow speakers on Twitter.

Funding your courses
Funding is available to pay for your training and you can look into professional and career development loans, grants and bursaries and courses through learndirect.

To develop new skills to move into a new area you could …

Contact friends, family and others in your network, and offer help for free
In many industries you could offer to work for free. It can add some current detail to your CV and also lead to goodwill – you may get recommended.

Voluntary work
If you are out of work, use some of this time on voluntary work to enhance your CV and develop more skills. Offer help to a charity or non-profit organisation in your area.

This doesn't have to be in a charity shop, unless that's what you want, but there could be backroom work, computer systems or marketing that you could help with. But working in the shop can also help – you will meet people, and the people you meet will know people, so be helpful and they may want to help you too.

IN A NUTSHELL

You now understand the importance of development to staying employable. The need to demonstrate to a potential employer that we are focused on being the best we can be and that we don't rest on qualifications gained in the past. There is a wide variety of learning options and opportunities. Which of these are best for you?

I'd like you to review your career goals – to keep your job, to get a new job, or to get a promotion – and choose at least one activity to enhance your CV and to increase your chance of success. What will you choose?

ACTIVITY 38

BEFORE YOU MOVE ON

- Make a note of three key points you have learnt.
- Make a note of what is the top takeaway, for you, from this chapter.

- **Review your options and choose at leat one development activity to start this week.**

APPENDIX 1

SOME EMPLOYERS WHO WELCOME OLDER APPLICANTS

CARE

- Hendra House
- Lilian Faithfull Homes
- The Partnership in Care
- Woodford Home Care and Support Services
- Southport Home Instead Senior Care

CONSTRUCTION

- Nicholson-Roberts Co Ltd
- Clugston Group Ltd

EDUCATION

- Queen Alexandra College
- Epping Forest College
- Stoke on Trent College
- Wakefield College

FINANCIAL SERVICES

- The Nationwide Building Society – report that their annual turnover is 4% for older staff compared with 10% for younger workers. Recruits in their fifties and sixties stay an average of 13 years.

HEALTH

- ABM University Health Board (part of NHS Wales)
- Portsmouth Hospitals NHS Trust

HOSPITALITY

- JD Wetherspoon – report that older workers record low absences, a strong work ethic and commitment to the business.
- Marston's
- McDonald's UK – employ over 1,000 people who are 60+ and they say that they make a huge impact on customer satisfaction.

LOCAL AUTHORITIES

- Falkirk Council
- Hertfordshire County Council
- North Warwickshire Borough Council

MANUFACTURING

- Allevard Springs Ltd
- South West Forgemasters
- British Gas
- Ronseal
- Centrica PLC

POLICE

- West Midlands Police

RETAIL

- ASDA Stores Ltd
- B&Q – report that absenteeism generally is 39% lower among their older workers.
- The Co-operative Group
- John Lewis
- Marks & Spencer

TRANSPORT

- A.T. Brown (Coaches) Ltd – 'They're like gold dust. Their experience and flexibility would be hard and costly to replace.'
- First Group

This list was taken from a 2013 government publication: www.gov.uk/government/uploads/system/uploads/attachment_data/file/142752/employing-older-workers-case-studies.pdf.

APPENDIX 2

USEFUL LINKS

Chapter 3 What am I going to do?

The National Careers Service	http://bit.ly/NatCS
Bright Outlook	http://bit.ly/1Oita5A
Government publications	www.gov.uk/government/publications/jobs-and-skills-in-2030
	www.gov.uk/government/publications/careers-of-the-future
	http://bit.ly/1Iq24GY
If you are based in the Midlands	www.futuresadvice.co.uk/lmi.html
If you are based in Northern Ireland	www.nidirect.gov.uk/job-trends.htm

Chapter 4 Why should I get the job?

The Big Five Personality Test	http://personality-testing.info/tests/BIG5.php

Chapter 8 21st-century CVs

Word clouds	www.tagcrowd.com
	www.worditout.com
	www.wordle.net

Chapter 9 LinkedIn and social media

Jackalope Jobs	www.jackalopejobs.com

Chapter 10 Promoting yourself and being found

Business cards	http://uk.moo.com
Alltop	http://alltop.com
Weebly – free website	www.weebly.com

Chapter 12 Traditional job search

Indeed	www.indeed.co.uk
Simplyhired	www.simplyhired.com
Careerjet.co.uk	www.careerjet.co.uk
vacancycentral.co.uk	www.vacancycentral.co.uk
LinkedIn profile rating	www.linkedin.com/wvmx/profile
Google Alerts	http://google.co.uk/alerts
Gumtree	www.gumtree.com/jobs
Craigslist	www.craigslist.org
Glassdoor	www.glassdoor.co.uk
TheJobCrowd	www.thejobcrowd.com
TARGETjobs	https://targetjobs.co.uk
Kompass	http://gb.kompass.com/b/business-directory/

Chapter 13 Alternatives to a permanent full-time job

Upwork	www.upwork.com
PeoplePerHour	www.peopleperhour.com/freelance/uk
Fiverr	www.fiverr.com
Craigslist	http://craigslist.org or e.g. http://bristol.craigslist.co.uk
Flexjobs	www.flexjobs.com
Guru	www.guru.com
Gumtree	www.gumtree.com/jobs

Chapter 15 Staying motivated

Meet up	www.meetup.com

Chapter 16 How to stay employable

TED talks	www.ted.com/talks
The Open Education Consortium	www.oeconsortium.org/courses/
Coursera	www.coursera.org
YouTube	www.youtube.com
iTunes podcasts	www.apple.com/uk/itunes/podcasts/discover
edX – free courses	www.edx.org
OU free courses	www.open.edu/openlearn/free-courses

Volunteering

www.do-it.org.uk

www.volunteering.org.uk

www.reachskills.org.uk

More

www.prime.org.uk – PRIME was established by HRH The Prince of Wales in response to letters he was receiving from people desperate to work but unable to find anyone to employ them because of their age.

www.saga.co.uk

www.laterlife.com

http://age-net.co.uk

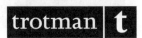